ARCHITECTURAL DESIGN

EDITORIAL OFFICES:
42 LEINSTER GARDENS, LONDON W2 3AN
TEL: 071-402 2141 FAX: 071-723 9540

HOUSE EDITOR: Maggie Toy EDITORIAL TEAM: Nicola Hodges, Ramona Khambatta, Katherine MacInnes
SENIOR DESIGNER: Andrea Bettella
DESIGN CO-ORDINATOR: Mario Bettella
DESIGN TEAM: Gregory Mills, Jaqueline Grosvenor, Owen Thomas,

CONSULTANTS: Catherine Cooke, Terry Farrell, Kenneth Frampton, Charles Jencks, Heinrich Klotz, Leon Krier, Robert Maxwell, Demetri Porphyrios, Kenneth Powell, Colin Rowe, Derek Walker

SUBSCRIPTION OFFICES.
UK: VCH PUBLISHERS (UK) LTD
8 WELLINGTON COURT, WELLINGTON STREET
CAMBRIDGE CB1 1HZ UK

USA: VCH PUBLISHERS INC
303 NW 12TH AVENUE DEERFIELD BEECH,
FLORIDA 33442-1788 USA

ALL OTHER COUNTRIES:
VCH VERLAGSGESELLSCHAFT MBH
BOSCHSTRASSE 12, POSTFACH 101161
D-6940 WEINHEIM GERMANY

© 1993 *Academy Group Ltd.* All rights reserved. No part of this publication may be reproduced or transmitted in any form or by any means, electronic or mechanical, including photocopying, recording or any information storage or retrieval system without permission in writing from the Publishers. Neither the Editor nor the Academy Group hold themselves responsible for the opinions expressed by writers of articles or letters in this magazine. The Editor will give careful consideration to unsolicited articles, photographs and drawings; please enclose a stamped addressed envelope for their return (if required). Payment for material appearing in AD is not normally made except by prior arrangement. All reasonable care will be taken of material in the possession of AD and agents and printers, but they regret that they cannot be held responsible for any loss or damage. *Subscription rates for 1993 (including p&p)*: Annual rate: UK only £59.00, World DM 185, USA $120.00 Student rate: UK only £45.00, World DM 149, USA $100.00. Individual issues: £12.95/DM 35.00 (plus £2.30/DM 5 for p&p, per issue ordered), US$24.95 (incl p&p). Printed in Singapore. All prices are subject to change without notice. [ISSN: 0003-8504]

CONTENTS

ARCHITECTURAL DESIGN **MAGAZINE**

Sidney K Robinson The Continuous Present of Organic Architecture • *Site Specific* Energetic Architecture • Books • Exhibitions

ARCHITECTURAL DESIGN **PROFILE** No 104

VISIONS FOR THE FUTURE

Jean **Nouvel** Tomorrow Can Take Care of Itself • *Michael* **Davies** Changes in the Rules • *Guy* **Battle** and *Christopher* **McCarthy** Multi-Source Synthesis • *Hans* **Helms** The City Shaken • *Maxwell* **Hutchinson** Rethinking the Future • *Michael* **Spens** The National Writing Centre and City Library, Swansea • **Alsop & Störmer** • *Richard* **Rogers** Partnership • *Norman* **Foster** and Partners • **V**on **Gerkan**, Marg and Partners • *Santiago* **Calatrava** • **Future Systems** • *Peter* **Pran** of *Ellerbe Becket and Michael Fieldman* • *Hajime* **Yatsuka** • *Yasufumi* **Kijima** • *Kiko* **Mozuna**

James T Hubbell, Vint House, Del Mar

Bart Prince, Bart Prince Residence

Alsop & Störmer, National Centre for Literature, Swansea

THE CONTINUOUS PRESENT OF ORGANIC ARCHITECTURE
SIDNEY K ROBINSON

The 'Continuous Present of Organic Architecture' exhibition, organised by the Contemporary Art Centre Cincinnati, Ohio early in 1991, was an attempt to demonstrate what 'organic' architecture might be. A group of six architects with overlapping ideals represent a distinctive branch of American organic architecture that begins with Louis Sullivan (1856-1924) continues with Walter Burley Griffin (1876-1937) and Bruce Goff (1904-1982), and flourishes presently through two of Goff's students, Herb Greene and Bart Prince, and Cincinnati architect Terry Brown. These six were chosen not as a claim for exclusive, but representative and notable membership in the lineage.

The search begins by setting aside the accumulated claims for the natural, the functional and the ecological made by its various interpreters. For some, organic is curved, organic is asymmetrical, organic is natural materials, organic is individualistic, organic is holistic, organic is not mechanical, organic is good. These assertions drift vaguely between a specific style and an indefinite concept that takes on many different forms. This exhibition momentarily parts this tangle of notions so that yet another try can be made at sighting the elusive phenomenon of organic architecture.

The 'continuous present' is a phrase from Gertrude Stein that Bruce Goff quoted to identify this important characteristic of the work:

> Everything is the same except composition and as the composition is different and always going to be different everything is not the same. So then I as a contemporary creating the composition in the beginning was groping toward a continuous present, a using everything, a beginning again and again.

Immediate activity, both creation and perception, is a primary value in this architecture. Direct expression rather than laborious calculation gives the appearance of spontaneity, which is, in fact, supported by an energetic exploration.

Organic architecture is a Dionysian force upsetting the control of reason and the propriety of convention. It does not reject them, but employs reason for its power to challenge, and convention for its ability to encourage participation. When organic architecture acts as a corrective, it liberates the present from the dead hand of the past. If it is carried away in an excess of self-indulgence, it can destroy tradition by an assault of sensory stimulation. Along with other avant-garde movements, it continuously challenges the dominant culture. From that marginal position, it remains vital; accepted into the mainstream, it quickly becomes superficial.

Organic architecture does not simply turn away from the past in a fit of 'I'd rather do it myself'. The past, after all, is made up of a series of what were once 'presents'. Immortality is not sought in a frozen image, but through individual re-enactment. Organic architecture lives through its immediate impact and its potential to continuously delight, as well as to challenge. In some respects it is more like the recursive gestures of dance with its rhythm of movement, the sparkle of costumes and geometry of its platform or grotto. Constant re-creation separates it from other architectures that quickly move away from immediate circumstances to take refuge in representation, codification and analysis.

The biological proposition that ontogeny repeats phylogeny (development of the individual re-enacts the development of the species) may be the only thing that organic architecture shares with a more literal identification with nature. By emphasising immediate sensory stimulation to connect with primordial forms of bold geometry it leaps over more cautious architecture that requires reassurance and confirmation. The emphasis on present activity is shared with a radical rationalism that rejects the accumulation of tradition in favour the operations of the human mind acting in the present. Organic architecture could be considered the sensory correlative of a rationalist architecture.

The organic imagination is potentially wayward and uncontrollable. The architecture it produces is not simply licentious, whatever those who live next door may conclude. In the midst of this exuberant creation, the continuity of geometry guides the free exploration of the past and the joyful engagement with the present. Geometry is the one constant that transcends individual time and space. It is present always as if it were new. Its laws are forever being discovered by the excited individual working with straight edge and compass. Its wonder and mystery, traced from the workings of the cosmos, can only be obscured by appeals to convenience. Organic geometry is always much more than that.

The Organic of Louis Sullivan

The figure that serves as the reference point for subsequent developments in American organic architecture is Louis Sullivan. His writings, as well as his buildings and the ornament that adorns them,

James T Hubbell, OPPOSITE: Rainbow Hill; INSETS: Architect's own home (Photographer: Gene Faulkner)

III

remain today as primary sources. Because Frank Lloyd Wright (1867-1959) called Sullivan 'liebermeister' after working with him from 1888 to 1893 and referred to his own architecture as organic, Sullivan stands at the head of a self-identified lineage. Wright's genius and the brilliance of his self-presentation have obscured alternative approaches to organic architecture. These other facets, visible by looking aside from Wright, were the focus of the exhibition.

Louis Sullivan read the poetry of Walt Whitman and recommended it to this young apprentice Frank Lloyd Wright. Many Americans seeking to define what was unique about their nation were attracted to Whitman's sprawling energetic poetry. His emphasis on democracy has received much attention, but its importance lies in setting the context of a political system. The return to personal experience and individual action always risks anarchy even as it strives toward a new kind of order. Whitman's 'Song of Myself' (1855) can be innocently read as a call for natural freedom and individual self-fulfilment. But in the opening stanzas an important context for such free explorations is clearly set: 'Creeds and schools in abeyance,/Retiring back a while suffices at what they are but never forgotten'.

These creeds and schools concentrated the diffused raw material of their own times in their books, paintings, architecture. 'Houses and rooms are full of perfumes, the shelves are crowded with perfumes,/ I breathe the fragrance myself and know it and like it,/ The distillation would intoxicate me also, but I shall not let it'. The self that does not take 'things at second or third hand' as it goes on its journey of exploration is not innocent, naive or native. It simply wants to distill things for itself.

Whitman's journey in search of 'the origin of all poems' appears to require no baggage, but is, in fact, laden with accumulated experiences transmitted through the convention of words. The paradox of pushing convention aside even as one employs it is only a seeming contradiction, whether in poetry or in architecture. Whitman is not so simple as to forget that 'these are really the thoughts of all men in all ages and lands, they are not original with me'.

Organic architecture struggles to keep up the pressure of vivid individual experience in the face of tradition. The received wisdom of tradition seeks domination through the manoeuvres of cultural politics that dispense commissions, recognition and propriety. Democracy in this context is not so much a political system as the most dramatic setting in which to play out the contest between the part and the whole, the individual and the accumulated culture. This compositional emphasis on continuity and differentiation is what makes the discussion of democracy an architectural subject.

Sullivan's organic asserts the rights of a unique identity, citizen or building, even as it recognises its responsibility to contribute to the community of shared interest of which it is a part. Bart Prince and Terry Brown are more representative of the claims of unique identity and Herb Greene has come to be more concerned with the responsibility to the whole.

Following on Whitman's opening qualification of the isolated individual in 'Song of Myself', Sullivan establishes the status of the individual enterprise in the 'living present' as 'firm-rooted in the past' even as it 'takes on local colour of identity'. His ideal is not to lose the identity, or to subordinate it completely, but to differentiate it from the larger continuity. 'The active resistance continually meets th[e] ceaseless, aspiring force' as the organic architect merges only for an inspired moment, 'for the time being with the identity or inner nature of other things'. This is as true of the parts of a building, such as the ornament, as it is true of the individual man who 'is a law unto himself' but not lawless. The desire to let the part or the man break free keeps upsetting any comfortably consistent composition. It makes Sullivan's architecture difficult in ways that are reminiscent of his onetime employer Frank Furness of Philadelphia.

The distinctive difference between Sullivan's and Wright's idea of organic architecture depends on whether organic is taken to mean multiple and varied or singular and integral. Although Sullivan uses the singular definition from time to time, he characteristically introduces the democratic ideal to give organic a multiple face, just as his buildings are made of distinct elements, differentiated, but not subordinated, to a singular idea. Wright, in his early career, emphasised the singularly focused integration that he had picked up from Sullivan's ornament.

Frank Lloyd Wright interpreted Louis Sullivan in a peculiar way. Wright was quite clear that what he learned from Sullivan came from his ornament, not his architecture as a whole. Wright did not make buildings in response to Sullivan's buildings. He made architecture from the principles he discerned in a part of those buildings. Wright reflected that he came to know 'that many a long lifetime must be spent to find the proper technique – each man for himself – to put into actual building practice the implications of the great philosophy to which the lyric poet dedicated himself in this sensuous efflorescence so peculiarly and absolutely his own.' Wright's early attempts to make the interpretative leap that developed a whole building out of the ornamental part of a building were not successful: Ansh Maariav is still in Chicago on South Michigan Avenue to attest to the folly of the experiments I made in violent changes of scale in actual building construction as I had seen lieber-meister practice in ornament with startling success.' By looking sympathetically at Sullivan's ornament, Wright had seized on an interpretation of integrity within the building itself and/or continuous with its setting in the natural world. 'Many years later as I lived, drew and built I

Bart Prince, ABOVE: Whiting Residence, Sun Valley, Idaho; BELOW: Detail of roof (Photographers: Allan Weintraub and Kirk Gittings)

found in what I conceived and drew the element I now call plasticity (the master had rendered it so completely in clay) carried in its own nature implications of previously unexplored structural continuity.'

This unique reading of Sullivan's organic immediately suggests that other readings could take into account the whole of Sullivan's way of making architecture. On the matter of ornament, for instance, Sullivan states clearly it was to be like the building on which it was found, but it was independent in some way as well. He takes care to point out that ornament for instance, Sullivan states clearly it was to be like the building in which it was found, but it was independent in some way as well. He takes care to point out that ornament, while sympathetic to the spirit that animates the mass, does not appear to receive that spirit, but to express it by virtue of differential growth.' This is a fine point, but a crucial one. It leaves open the possibility for a distinctive differentiation, a unique expression by the ornament, or the part, itself.

For Wright, organic suggested more of the subordination that Sullivan would accept in his buildings or in his ideal of democracy. A different kind of integration produced Wright's Unity Temple (1906), and Sullivan's Merchants National Bank in Grinnell, Iowa (1914). The differences between the ornamental window over the bank's front door and the slender metal columns in the large side window would be unacceptable to Wright. Wright worked long and hard to bring the ornamentation of Unity Temple's exterior columns into geometric concordance with the building as a whole. The differences between the parts of Sullivan's bank and their relationship to the simple brick block of the building, demonstrate the difficult balance Sullivan was trying to establish in contrast to the subordinating continuity enforced by Wright.

In so far as Wright is considered a source for canonical modernism, he is organic in a very traditional sense. Most of his early work fits into a venerable architectural tradition of tightly integrated compositions. His later work, often troubling to traditional modernists, is more organic as he progressively loosens the bonds of integration to let divergent parts slide in his multiple geometries. The 'Continuous Present' exhibition established a viable alternative reading of organic: traditional in its preference for centralising geometries, non-traditional in its incorporation of geometric patterns, colours and materials that are not subordinated to an obviously dominant architectural expression. Wright's organic can be read, in contrast, as traditional in its effort to make thoroughly integrated buildings and non-traditional in its pursuit of de-centred, sliding compositions. Wright generally chooses to express the self-conscious conventions of community with an obviously centralised arrangement, while the looser adjustments of the vernacular appear in his domestic work.

The wall and ceiling paintings of Sullivan's Home Building Association building in Newark, Ohio (1914), are striking examples of large surfaces intensified by ornament. Their place on the upper planes of the simple, rectangular room respects the larger spatial geometries, but their energy and boldness, like the exterior ornament express an independent growth, not a respectful subordination. In these murals Sullivan enlarges the generally diminutive geometric framework of previous ornament to the scale of the building as a whole, much as he did in the ornament around the front window at the Grimmell bank from the same year. This enlargement creates a tense balance between the simple, compact volume and it wrapping by a nearly competing surface geometry. The contrast between material and geometry creates an organic architecture of challenging vehemence rather than comforting coherence.

Sullivan's 'System of Architectural Ornament' drawn in 1922 is the most compelling demonstration of an organic ideal based on a compact geometric identity ornamented by an independent foliated efflorescence. Sullivan posits an initial centre or 'seed' with its projected axes and then elaborates them with stunning imagination. Whenever the centrifugal forces tend to break loose, a geometric centre is re-established.

The ornament's independent expression of the architectural spirit is crucial to this architecture. Sullivan's interest in Owen Jones' *Grammar of Ornament* (1856) and his exposure at the Beaux Arts academy in 1874 to a non-classical system of ornament, reinforce the significance of the development of his own ornament. Another important figure is Gottfried Semper, known in Chicago through translations at the turn of the century, whose proposals of a textile origin for architecture evolved in a comparable fashion. Semper's 'dressing' of an elemental core form in the symbolic rhythms of dance and music seems a description of this organic architecture. The contemporary Viennese art historian Otto Antonia Graf has developed in the last decade a powerful speculation on how the plane of ornamental geometry unfolds from the enclosing gesture of a caressing hand. His brilliant link between the body of the building and the ornamental intensification of the building, makes his 'Die Kunst des Quadrats' (1983) a crucial text for organic architecture.

An American Organic Architecture

The 'Continuous Present' exhibition of American organic architecture locates the beginning of architecture in a singular, centred identity. This identity, as made clear by the poet Whitman and the architect Sullivan, is manifest both in an individual citizen and in a building. The centre claimed and sustained by the individual building is often a compact geometric form, singular or linked in a series, that confirms the human dimension. The

Terry Brown, ABOVE: A bird feeder and six lamps for Lib Stone, Cincinnati, Ohio

simple form, angled or circular, stands clear even when its outline is animated by the ornament that borders or envelopes it. The disposition of ornament in Sullivan's banks and mausolea is a clear demonstration of this principle.

The compact centre is an origin that architecture has always claimed. The classical evolution of architecture from hearth to house to temple, extended by Renaissance and Beaux Arts precepts, has similar roots. However, this tradition differs significantly from the organic in its obedient acceptance of reports about the beginning of architecture and in its obsessive preservation of the record of those reports. Organic architecture is driven by a more reckless and youthful desire to see for itself how architecture begins. It is this youthfulness that makes it seem so quintessentially American to foreign observers. The American experience of settling a new land, new in so far as it was unspoiled by European pride, emphasised beginnings and individual discovery in the late nineteenth century . . . The freshness of the origin is evident in the way materials are chosen and used. Because organic architecture does not yearn for acceptance in traditional terms, it seems intentionally to choose materials that lie outside the canon of proper architectural materials. The impact of these unexpected materials can be perceived as both awkward and delightful. These materials can be either natural in origin, but used in a particularly aggressive way, or they can be manufactured parts that are rarely thought of in an architectural context. Coal, goose feathers and tile vie with mirror, perforated metals screens or ashtrays . . .

Organic architecture steps forward in a world of caution and compromise to take personal responsibility for its energy and its invitation to individual freedom. It draw together memories, desires and dreams and brings forth architecture that forcefully engages a specific present. It takes spatial volumes and measures them out in regular units as a continuation of ancient and original forms, but on the surfaces and edges of these concentrated units, it traces ornamental rhythms of great freedom and vividness. It addresses the future not with the heavy feet that produced the pyramids, seeking justification by outlasting time itself, but with the recursive movement of the regenerative cycles of living species.

Extract from Sidney K Robinson's article for the catalogue of the exhibition 'The Continuous Present of Organic Architecture', Contemporary Arts Center, Cincinnati, Ohio. He is featured in the forthcoming issue of Architectural Design.

Bart Prince, LEFT: Detail of Prince Residence, Albuguerque, New Mexico; OPPOSITE: Exterior view, (Photographer: Kirk Gittings)

ENERGETIC ARCHITECTURE
SITE SPECIFIC

Site Specific is the collaboration of a sculptor, Nicholas Kirkham and an architectural student Gordon Shrigley. They have a dialectical approach which allows a discussion between art and architecture. It centres on installation art and the way in which built form provokes, informs and responds to users and passers-by. Their work addresses broader global concerns; ideas of living in the city, the exploitation of the Earth's resources and the needs of the future. Site Specific's latest provocative work, the 147 Project, is a proposal to insert three self-contained dwelling units into a disintegrating Victorian Building. The site is mid-terrace on Ladbroke Grove in West London and is adjacent to the elevated section of a six lane motorway, the Westway. The proximity between the Westway and the site is seen as an active part of the programme. Site Specific endeavour to evoke an analogy between watching the river from the bank of the Thames and lying on the slope of the installation looking at the Westway.

The proposal involves stripping the inner structure of the building to remove all traces of previous intentions, leaving only a hollowed-out shell. The interior is reformed by the insertion of a single object that inhabits the shell. As the body of this rises through the structure it twists towards the sun. The object itself is constructed out of timber, using boat building technology to create a monocoque structure, built up of strips of laminated wood that will allow the skin to work with the twist. This is held in space by beams that span the gap between the party walls. The roof is a softly curved deck that invites occupants to lie upon its slope and contemplate their surroundings.

Contained within the object are the three dwelling units, which are denoted by timber floor planes set within the internal limits of the object. The margin between these limits and the shell is spanned by glass, the transparency of this bridge allows light to pour down the sides, defining an inner core. This permits the inhabitants to view the installation from inside and out. The volume of the object is cut and a slit of opaque glass permits light to penetrate, casting shadows of occupancy from within the core. The open connection between private and public space through the transparent glass boarder of the flat's floor, illicits a response – a self-conscious reaction. This space relies on the sensitivity of the individual to their surroundings, questioning the performance of domestic living. The drama of these events is emphasised by the glass floor hidden behind the entrance to each unit, at the moment of opening the door the solidity of the floor dissolves suspending expectation.

The re-ordering of the internal space by the exposure of the building's section reveals the character of the installation and its relationship with the remaining mute Victorian Facade, reinforcing the schism between previous and future intentions. The stripping of Victorian excesses and the restraints of claustrophobic planning, create a *tabula rasa*. The installation, with its 'living planes' and non-prescriptive use, can be seen as raw potential – 'a table that may be laid for any occasion'. The significance of the notion of shared experience – between interior and exterior, between inhabitant and passer-by – is essential to the concept of communality.

It has become apparent that the needs of the future must be considered in terms of ecological welfare, and with this in mind Site Specific has worked closely with Ove Arup to produce schemes that are consciously energy efficient. The balance between technology, form and building fabric, is designed to enhance the quality of the space, relying on passive rather than active systems to take advantage of free natural resources. The roof of the object is a solar attic, using its margin as a buffer zone that moderates the effects of heat loss and heat gain. The articulation of these intentions informs the narrative and is interwoven into the whole concept, not merely applied to the surface.

147 is a relatively modest small-scale project, as the opportunites to build experimental projects today are limited. However, with the collaboration and sponsorship of the building industries and related professions, the task of building this project within an extremely tight budget is eased. This has also forced a questioning of the processes of building which seems to require a knowledge of products that are prescriptive in use, rather than an innate sense of the materiality of things. 147 is the product of a collaboration of individuals motivated by a desire to create and a commitment to the exploration of ideas that would be difficult to develop within a more commercially led project. The building work itself is completed in the same manner with details designed and crafted on site.

Kaye Heron

Site Specific: Nicholas Kirkham and Gordon Shrigley, Kaye Heron, Philip Richards, Raymond Shotter in collaboration with Ove Arup and Battle & McCarthy.

MAIN PICTURE AND INSET BELOW: Concept model; INSET ABOVE: Exhibition centre

THE HENRY MOORE INSTITUTE

On 21st April, the Henry Moore Institute in Leeds, a £5 million International Centre for Sculpture, was officially opened. Designed by the internationally acclaimed architects Jeremy Dixon and Edward Jones in partnership with BDP, the building provides a unique centre in Europe for the display, study, research and promotion of sculpture of all periods and nationalities. The Institute occupies 20,000 square feet of space on four floors, including one of the first modern galleries designed exclusively for sculpture in Europe, together with study facilities, offices and storage space.

The Institute occupies three converted 19th-century wool merchants' offices at the end of Cookridge Street. The existing buildings are domestic in character with elevations looking onto Cookridge Street and Alexander Street. The conversion had to strike a balance between the retention of existing structure and the particular needs of a sculpture institute.

The four storey buildings naturally divide vertically to give galleries at upper ground floor served by storage and plant rooms at lower ground floor. This leaves the first floor as a study centre and the second floor for administration. The only new building is the main gallery space created by filling in the existing courtyard to Alexander Street. A bridge links the existing Leeds City Art Gallery to the new Institute at first floor level.

The sculpture galleries are simple white spaces with a minimum of detail. Their character comes from the quality of daylight and the contrasting scales of the spaces available within the existing structures. The study centre and administration floor are detailed in a different manner from the galleries, using natural oak in order to give a relaxed environment in which to work.

The entrance takes the form of a minimalist sculptural idea using the mechanical repetition of flights of steps generated as the ground falls across the frontage, together with a stone wall placed against the end of the terrace to leave explicit the cut. The whole entrance structure is made of granite used in its various natural forms. The vertical surfaces are all polished and the horizontal surfaces are all 'flamed' to give a contrasting texture. A tall eccentrically placed slot in the polished wall marks the entrance behind which is the shallow stepped passage that leads to the galleries. The elevation of the new gallery filling in the courtyard is intended to look less permanent than the surrounding brick structure. It consists of a grid of bronze frames filled with natural oak and obscure glass and incorporates a pair of giant doors to give access for larger sculptures.

Photographs by Richard Bryant/ARCAID

BOOKS

BOOKS RECEIVED:

CONNECTIONS: STUDIES IN BUILDING ASSEMBLY by Alan J Brookes and Chris Grech, Butterworth Heinemann, Oxford, 1992, 128pp, b/w ills, HB £37.50

DECANTATIONS: A TRIBUTE TO MAURICE CRAIG by Agnes Bernelle, The Lilliput Press, Dublin, 1992, 250pp, b/w ills, HB £35.00

DESIGN WORKS COMPANION by Janice Whale, Sigma Press, Wilmslow, 1993, 252pp, b/w ills, PB £14.95

ARCHITECTURE AND IDEOLOGY IN EASTERN EUROPE DURING THE STALIN ERA: AN ASPECT OF COLD WAR HISTORY by Anders Åman, MIT Press, London, 284pp, b/w ills, HB £31.50

VALUE PRICING FOR THE DESIGN FIRM by Frank A Stasiowski, John Wiley & Sons, 1993, 218pp, HB £34.95

AIA ARCHITECTRUAL GUIDE TO NASSAU AND SUFFOLK COUNTIES, LONG ISLAND by the American Institute of Architects, Long Island Chapter, and The Society for the Preservation of Long Island Antiquities, Constable Publishers, 1993, 206pp, b/w ills, PB £14.95

DIE STADT DER 500 000: NS-STADTPLANUNG UND ARCHITEKTUR IN WILHELMSHAVEN by Ingo Sommer, Vieweg, 1993, 438pp, b/w ills, HB DM 98

JAN DUIKER Works and Projects by Jan Molema, Editorial Gustavo Gili, 1989, 206pp, b/w ills, PB price N/A

ARCHITECTURAL WORKING DRAWINGS Residential and Commercial Buildings by Wiliam P Spence, John Wiley & Sons, 1993, 522pp, b/w ills, HB £41.95

STRENGTH OF MATERIALS AND STRUCTURES with an Introduction to Finite Element Methods by John Case, Lord Chilver and Carl TF Ross, Edward Arnold, 3rd ed 1993, 502p ills, PB £19.95

SKETCHES AND MEASURINGS DANISH ARCHITECTS IN GREECE 1818-1862 by Margit Bendtsen, Aahus University Press, 1993, 384pp, b/w and col ills, price N/A

Margit Bendtsen presents the studies made by Danish architects in their rediscovery of Greek architecture during the first half of the 19th century, upon the decline and fall of the Ottoman Empire. Winckelmann had stated in 1764 that the finest works of art were produced in Athens in the 5th and 4th centuries BC, when freedom and democracy prevailed, and that the masterpieces from this period should serve as models and inspiration for contemporary neo-classical art. But European architects had no accurate representations of Greek buildings to refer to until the society of Antiquities sent James Stuart and Nicholas Revett to measure and describe the monuments of ancient Greece in 1751-55. Their work *The Antiquities of Athens* meant that neo-classical architects no longer had to rely on Roman models and a steady flow of scholars began to travel to Greece.

Among these early scholars were two Danes, Peter Oluf Brøndsted and Georg Koës, whose important excavations (made with CR Cockerell among others) were published and provided many other Danes with the inspiration to travel. It is the work of these, of Jørgen Hansen Koch, Christian and Theophilos Hansen, M Gottlieb Bindesbøll, Niels Sigfred Nebelong, Laurits Albert Winstrup, Harald Conrad Stilling and Ferdinand Meldahl that Bendtsen discusses, showing that not only did they study, measure document, and excavate ruins, but that they also practiced as architects in the rebuilding of Athens. Bendsen provides succinct biographies on each architect's activities in Greece and proceeds to discuss the Greek monuments, details, Byzantine churches and Turkish architecture studied by these scholars. There follows a catalogue of the superb watercolours and carefully measured drawings which they produced, many never published before.

MIES VAN DER ROHE: BARCELONA PAVILION by Ignasi de Sola-Morales, Cristian Cirici and Fernando Ramos, Editorial Gustavo Gili, Barcelona, 72pp, b/w and col ills, price N/A

Mies van der Rohe's Pavilion was designed for the Barcelona International Exposition which eventually took place in 1929, having been delayed by the Great War, and was dismantled in 1930. From 1981-86 a team of architects embarked on the complex research and reconstruction of the structure.

Originally the industries of the participating countries were accommodated together in a series of grand palaces laid out around the great avenue ascending from the Plaza de Espana to the Palau Nacional building. It was decided in 1927, however, that countries should also build their own national pavilions, and it was to fulfil this function that Mies van der Rohe designed his German pavilion.

The book is described by the

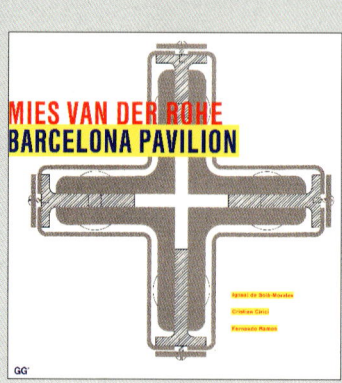

authors as 'little more than the design report of our project'. Divided into two sections, the first provides an extensive historical survey of the many design changes, the materials and critical reaction to the 1929 pavilion. Old photographs show the original building process and the *ad hoc* method of construction, while in the second section beautiful colour plates show the splendour of the reconstruction. They convey the vigorous geometry, the precision cut stone, marble, glass and steel and the clarity of assembly for which the pavilion has become famous. Also illustrated and discussed is the 'Barcelona' furniture of tubular steel which has become so renowned. A building originally designed as a modest pavilion is confirmed in its status as a paradigm of 20th-century architecture.

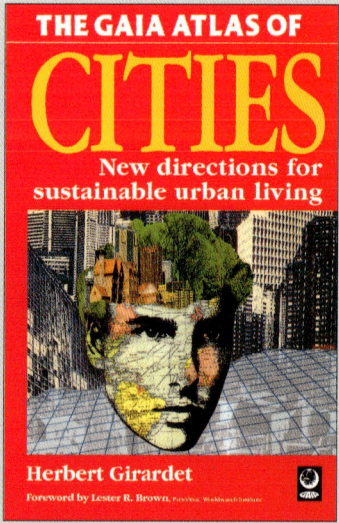

THE GAIA ATLAS OF CITIES New Directions for Sustainable Living by Herbert Giradet, Gaia Books, London, 1993, 192pp, col ills, £9.99

This is a timely book coming in the wake of the Rio Conference which – while somewhat neglecting the plight of cities – called for a major drive to make cities more sustainable. The cultural ecologist, author and television producer Herbert Giradet writes on the reconciliation of 'human kind and its host planet'. He views cities, the most complex product of the human mind, as huge organisms. He looks beyond the static structures of stone and concrete to their active metabolisms, to their consumption of food, fuels and raw materials and their production of waste and pollution.

While 50 per cent of the population now live in cities the ramifications go still further, 75 per cent of resources are consumed by cities and their demands for commodities such as tropical hardwoods means that the tentacles of their demands penetrate yet further. Giradet argues that the linear metabolism of cities, of their consumption of raw materials and production of waste, must be reorganised to a circular one. He urges an environmental accountancy, where balance sheets

BOOKS

BOOKS RECEIVED:

HERZOG & DE MEURON *introduction by José Luis Mateo, Editorial Gustavo Gili, 1989, 96pp, b/w ills, PB price N/A*

M LAPENA/TORRES *introduction by Peter Buchanan and José Quetglas, Editorial Gustavo Gili, 1990, 96pp, b/w ills, PB price N/A*

SHOWROOMS AND EXHIBITION DISPLAY *2 produced by Nobuo Momose, Meisei Publications, 1992, 224pp, col ills, price N/A*

THE INTERNATIONAL DESIGN YEARBOOK *edited by Rick Poynor, Laurence King Publishing, 1993, 240pp, col ills, HB £39*

MAPPING THE FUTURES Local Cultures, Global change *edited by Jon Bird, Barry Curtis, Tim Putnam, George Robertson and Lisa Tickner, Routledge, 1993, 288pp, b/w ills, PB £11.99*

SIGNS OF OUR TIME *by John Margolies and Emily Gwathmey, Abbeville Press, 1993, 96p, col ills, HB £13.95*

AN ENGLISH ARCADIA Landscape Architecture in Britain and America, *papers delivered at a Huntington Symposium by Harriet Ritvo, Stephen Bending, Therese O'Malley, Stephen Daniels, Peter Mandler, George Clarke, Peter Inskip and Richard Wheeler, Huntingdon Library Press, 534ppp, b/w ills, PB £20*

THE OFFICIAL LONDON TRANSPORT GUIDE TO ALL LONDON MUSUEMS *by the London Museums Service, 1993, 78pp, b/w ills, PB £3.50*

THE COMPUTER ARTIST'S HANDBOOK Concepts, Techniques and Applications *by Lilian F Schwartz with Laurens R Schwartz, Norton, 1993, 318pp, HB £35*

DESKTOP DESIGN: Getting the professional look, *second edition, by Brian Chapman Chapman & Hall, March 1993, 126pp, b/w ills, PB £19.95*

of input and output are compiled (so far only done for Hong Kong). He looks at problems of water and food supply and wastage, at the reduction of energy consumption, and at the recycling of human and animal waste to provide phosphates. Always offering global case studies he shows how Third World cities are actually more efficient at waste recycling and sorting than their western counterparts, and how German cities have revolutionised domestic and industrial energy supply through combined heat and power plants.

The first section of the book deals with the ecology of settlements and their growth to city status, the second examines 'sick cities' and 'the city as parasite' while the concluding chapter looks at 'healing the city' by examining 'real people', their requirements and wishes, and proposing ideas for the 'responsible city'.

BONELL & GIL-RIUS, introduction by Jacques Lucan, Editorial Gustavo Gili, 1993, 96pp, b/w ills, price N/A

This catalogue focuses on the work of Esteve Bonell and his collaboration with Josep M Gil and Francesc Rius. While Bonell and Gil have shared an office in Barcelona since 1977, collaboration between Bonell and Rius has been on the basis of individual projects such as the Velodrom de Horta cycle track in Barcelona (1983-84) and the Municipal Sports Pavilion in Barcelona (1987-91) which was awarded the Mies van der Rohe Pavilion Prize for European Architecture 1992.

Precision and legibility characterise all Bonell's buildings. The design is never confused but always extremely subtle: the lines are taut, the surfaces clearly delimited, the volumes possess a comprehensible, if sometimes complex geometry, and there is always a rational ordering and articulation of the component parts. In his introduction Jacques Lucan discusses the evolution of Bonell's work through a number of different phases. Looking at the Fregoli I apartment building (1972-74) he explores ideas of space, at the Fregoli II building (1981-83) concepts of unity, at the Velodrom cycle track, the Masquefa school (1985-88) and Sant Esteve de ses Rovires penal institution (1986-91) ways of integrating the figure, and at the Girona Law Courts he concludes with the issue of public space.'The cultured observer,' writes Lucan, 'will find in his work a sensitive awareness of many other experiences in the history of architecture, yet without being able to point unequivocally to any excessively literal borrowing'.

THE GARDEN CITY Past, Present and Future edited by Stephen V Ward, E & FN Spon, 1992, 216pp, b/w ills, HB £39.95

The garden city was one of the most important and widespread ideas on planned urbanisation to emerge from the great period of town planning in the late 19th and early 20th centuries. Stephen Ward offers a reassessment of this movement which was not only a prelude to the new town programmes of the 1940s and 1960s but also constitutes a source of planning ideas of continuing relevance. The current rejection of modernism and continuing dissatisfaction with metropolitanism in much of the western world, in addition to mounting environmental concerns and the pursuit of sustainable urban development have pushed garden city thinking into the spotlight.

Here the reader is offered a critical and scholarly examination of the origins, implementation, international transference and adaption of the garden city concept. Stephen Ward has drawn together carefully selected contributions from internationally renowned scholars. Frederick Aalen discusses 'English Origins', Jean Pierre Gaudin writes on the French Garden City, Shun-ichi Watanabe on the Japanese aspect, Gerhard Fehl on the the Nazi Garden City, Robert Freestone on the Australian, Daniel Schaffer and Robert Fishman on the American and Michael Hebbert on the metamorphosis of the British Garden City, while Dennis Hardy provides an overview and postscript on the role of the garden city in the last decade of the 20th century.

THE QUALITY OF LEICESTER by Michael Taylor, Leicester City Council, 1993, 208pp, col ills, PB £14.95

'The problem of how to keep traditional towns alive, without destroying what makes life worth living in them, remains. There is no easy answer . . . but to love one's town and to learn everything one can about its history and what gives it individuality, is at least a step in the right direction.' (Mark Girouard, *The English Town*, 1990)

This is the cue which Leicester City Council has taken to produce a beautifully illustrated study of the history, areas, buildings and changing communities of Leicester. Aimed primarily at Leicester's residents and visitors the aim of the book is to reveal the rich, varied and individual character of the city. A picture of civic diversity and pride emerges.

XIII

EXHIBITIONS

APPLICATION & IMPLICATION – Modéle de pensée et acte de présence

The event is comprised of a seminar and a critical examination of 'Architecture au MAGASIN', an exhibition to be held at the Centre National d'Art Contemporain de Grenoble. The exhibition features the work of young European architects from different academic backgrounds presenting their ideas on the theme of 'Application and Implication' through the medium of an architectural object or installation. The exhibition accompanying the seminar features work by established architects such as Odile Decq and Enric Miralles.

'The status of architectural works like the organisation of space and architecture is a symptom of how small or large communities refer to themselves and situate themselves within space and time.' *Volume*, Sylviane Agacinski.

Each building has a double life, on one hand it is an independent element, on the other it is the place and/or the surface of a social act. A construction is at the same time a limit and an area of contact between society and architecture; paradoxically it divides and gathers. Shaped on and perceived through different concepts – symbolic, aesthetical, spatial and functional – a building is a consequence or an end of processes that are external, which isolate it from architecture. As such architecture appears submitted to a logic of the end.

Nevertheless the appropriation of a building is realised through the surface of its concept. The question is whether or not architecture 'serves' society. Do we have to consider architecture as an application for the remedy or the restructuring of society?

STRUCTURE SPACE AND SKIN, The Work of Nicholas Grimshaw & Partners 1988-1993

The drama of the British Pavilion at Expo 92 Seville and of the International Terminal at Waterloo is brought to London in this major exhibition which charts the work of Nicholas Grimshaw & Partners for the last five years.

The exhibition at Florence Hall, Royal Institute of British Architects, brings to life projects and major competition entries completed by the practice during the last five years and illustrates the diversity of approach and building type which now characterises its work. Dominating the show are mock-ups of two of the practice's most well known recent projects – a one third size section of the sail wall of the British Pavilion at Expo 92, and the top 7.5 metre section of one of the 'tusk' columns from the Western Morning News Building, its glazing arms reaching out into the air. Filling the space between these two mock-ups, and spilling out into the sculpture court, are more than 20 models, numerous full-size components and mock-ups of parts of buildings. Also included are models of major competition entries, for example the Bibliothéque in Paris and the model for a future airport, prepared for the 1991 Biennale of Architecture in Venice.

A range of models relating to the International Terminal at Waterloo, includes a detailed cutaway of the whole complex and a full size mock-up of the 'bow string' glazing system for the glass wall.

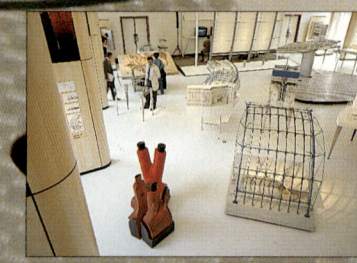

EXHIBITIONS

REILLY PRIZE – Excellence in Design Rewarded

As a pioneering director of the Design Council and later a trustee of the Design Museum, Lord Reilly was committed to a wider understanding of the nature of design in the general public and the business community. The objective of the Reilly Prize is to recognise excellence in design. The panel of judges includes Sir Terence Conran, Deyan Sudjic, Eva Jiricna and David Carter.

Earlier this year, the editorial team at *Blueprint Magazine* selected over 100 designs from around the world, ranging from 'Luna' Tadete wallcovering by Alessandro Mendini of RASCH and 'System 25' by the inhouse design team at Bulthaup to 'Soft Big Heavy Chair' by Ron Arad of Moroso SPA.

Apart from excellence in aesthetic approach, issues to be considered within the Reilly criteria are ecological and social responsibility, performance, measured against cost, innovation and visual longevity. Products and visuals of the entire Reilly Selection will be on display at Earls Court in a specially created exhibition space designed by Rasshied Din, interiors consultant to IDI.

The winner of the Reilly Prize will receive a specially commissioned Danny Lane award presented by the chairman of the judging panel, Sir Terence Conran and Lady Reilly.

CHICAGO ARCHITECTURE AND DESIGN, 1923-1993: Reconfiguration of an American Metropolis

This is the first major exhibition to comprehensively document and examine architectural changes in the American metropolis wrought by the cataclysmic events of the Great Depression of the 1930s and the Second World War, as well as the building booms of the 1920s, 1960s, and 1980s. Organised by John Zukowsky, curator of the Art Institute of Chicago's Department of Architecture, the exhibition consists of original drawings, paintings, prints comprising a gallery of works which includes 'For the Public Service' by Leslie Ragan which is a view of the La Salle Street Station and a Perspective Rendering of 120N Salle Street. The exhibition also includes architectural fragments and artefacts, furniture, furnishings, models, and photo murals; objects that explore and illuminate the transformation of the American urban landscape over the past seven decades.

An earlier exhibition focused on three key individuals in the heroic period of Chicago architectural history: Daniel H Burnham, Louis Sullivan, and Frank Lloyd Wright. This event explores a more complex period through installations arranged thematically around eight land-use, or building type categories found in today's cities.

These eight themed spaces are built of steel studs covered in wire mesh, left intentionally incomplete to reflect the process of building. Viewers traverse the spaces in a zig-zag pattern that directs them backwards in time from the present to the past.

REVIEWS

The magazine INOCULATES; the spectacle of the visual arts in perpetual retreat rests upon the determination of the magazine to arrest **all tendencies to direct action** in the realm of the visual.

FAT farts at these miserable organs of the innocuous.

In defiance we offer you *FAT* the first *GALAZINE* . . . ; the world's first *MAGAZERY*.

A collection of multiplicities, cross cuttings, re-readings, plagiarisms and samplings.
KR Rhowbotham c April 1993

This is an extract from the proposal for *Fat,* a magazine through which Kevin Rhowbotham 'damns' the present selection of architectural publications criticising them for using a 'moral tourniquet' to stem the 'free flow of ideas creating a market of artificial scarcity'. He claims that '*Fat*'s tactical procedures will forcefully dismember, re-aggregate and infect dominant taste cultures colonising them with their polar opponents to construct a nomadic, uncategorisable form . . .' We await the result with anticipation!

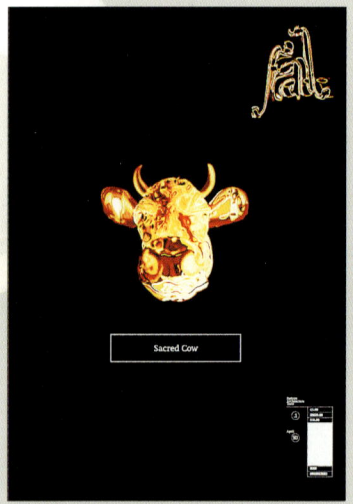

Places of the Soul, Architecture and Environmental Design as a Healing Art by Christopher Day
Published by Aquarian/Thorsons (an imprint of HarperCollins) 192pp, Paperback £9.99.

An incisive, positive examination of how we can reinstate the human factor in the building equation by allowing buildings to develop organically from people and place. The assertion is that our surroundings affect us physically and spiritually and that while personal preferences differ widely, there is a level of aesthetic response that we all share. Through this clearly written book Day articulates suspicions that we have all harboured in our subconscious. The first chapters analyse the problem using colourful historical examples. Architecture is potentially a dangerous tool that can be used to manipulate people, he sites the Nazi stadiums with their theatrical mood-distortion devices to argue that mood enhancement becomes manipulation when pressure is brought to bear.

He condemns the International Style for imposing generalisations regardless of what is appropriate for a particular place and the people of that place. Day concludes that architecture has such profound effects on human consciousness that it is far too important to bother with stylistic means of appealing to fashion.

The 'sick building syndrome' is the most extreme and widely recognised symptom of insensitive architecture, deriving from a combination of inadequate ventilation and microbiological, chemical, thermal and electrical dimensions.

Having analysed the problem he suggests ways of solving it, using very well captioned images to argue his case, starting with the most basic facets of perception such as the different effect of a straight line and a curve, acute and obtuse angles, smooth and irregular, textured surfaces.

Day advocates the 'ensouling' of buildings. through the sensitive juxtapostion of polar opposites. According to him, 'light and matter are the greatest of architectural polarities – the polarity of comos and substance, one bringing enlivening . . . rhythms and the other stable, enduring, rooted in place and time'.

He concludes, 'What I write is not novel; I write the obvious. It is my belief that we all already know it – and the test of my ability is whether you recognise truth in what I describe . . .'

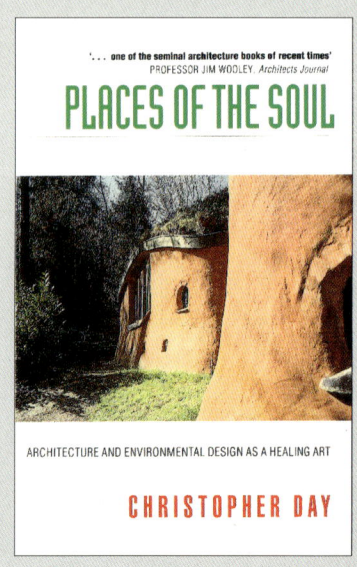

XVI

VISIONS FOR THE FUTURE

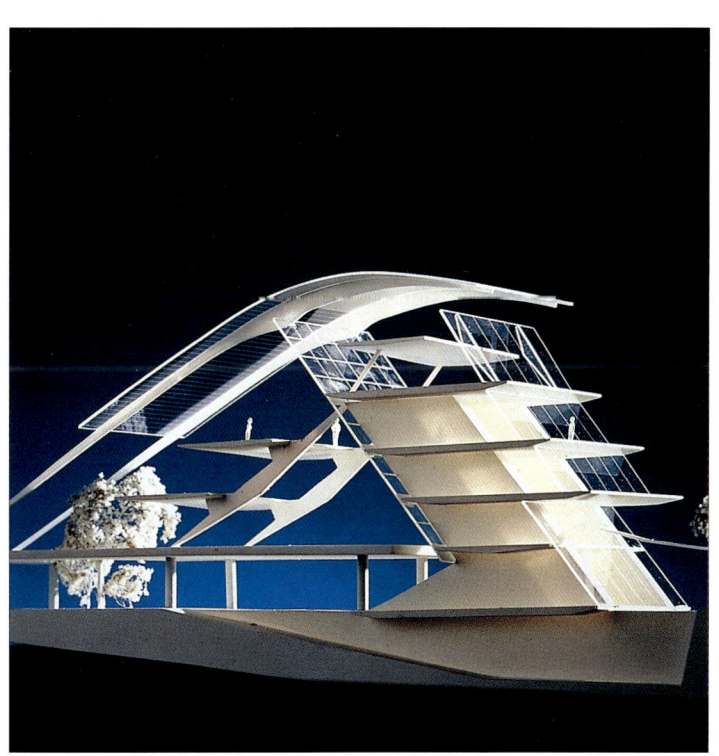

RICHARD ROGERS, VAL D'OISE

Architectural Design

VISIONS FOR THE FUTURE

ABOVE: ALSOP AND STÖRMER, CONCEPTUAL IMAGE OF TY LLEN, SWANSEA; *OPPOSITE*: RICHARD HORDEN ASSOCIATES, THE MILLENNIUM TOWER, GLASGOW, 'THE "WING" IS A RESPONSE TO NATURE – AN EXPRESSION OF A DESIRE TO LIVE AND DESIGN IN HARMONY WITH NATURE' (RICHARD HORDEN). THE WING IS AN AERODYNAMICALLY SHAPED TOWER MOUNTED ON MOTORS WHICH TURN IT ACCORDING TO THE PREVAILING WIND. IT RISES FROM A GLAZED AND GRANITE CIRCULAR BASE, UNDER WHICH THERE IS A RESTAURANT WHERE EACH TABLE HAS MIRROR TOPS ENCOURAGING VIEWS UP THE TOWER. THE SPACE ABOVE IS AN ARENA FOR POP CONCERTS ETC AND IT IS TOPPED BY A VIEWING PLATFORM.

ACADEMY EDITIONS • LONDON

Acknowledgements

All material is courtesy of the architects unless otherwise stated.
We would like to thank Guy Battle and Christopher McCarthy for their energy and enthusiasm in writing an essay especially for this issue; Michael Davies for giving us permission to publish an extract from his lecture 'Design Workshop Well-tempered Architecture', at the Technische Universität, Berlin, June 1991, text edited by Philipp Oswalt, first published in *ARCH +*, No 113, September 1992, Aachen; Hans Helms for the extract from his paper given at the sixth International Bauhaus Colloquium in Weimar, Germany, 18-20 June, 1992; Professor von Gerkan for permitting us to use extracts from the book *von Gerkan Marg & Partners*, Academy Editions, 1993; and to Johan Pijnappel for obtaining permission for us to use 'Tomorrow Can Take Care of Itself: A Conversation with Jean Nouvel' from *The Invisible in Architecture*, Academy Editions, 1993. We would also like to thank Kisho Kurokawa, the author of *New Wave Japanese Architecture*, Academy Editions, 1993 for allowing us to use material on Yasufumi Kijima and Kiko Mozuna

Front Cover: *Jean Nouvel, Galeries Lafayette, Berlin*
Back Cover: *Santiago Calatrava, Telephone Tower, Zurich, section*
Inside Front and Back Covers: *Kiko Mozuna, Shimokawa City Tower, Japan, interior*

Photographic Credits

Front cover and pp6-19 images courtesy of Jean Nouvel and the ICA, London; pp6, 13 Georges Fessy; p8 (top 3 insets), front cover and pp10, 12, 14 Berget Gaston; p8 (4th inset), p19 Quentin Bertoux; p17 (2nd inset) Olivier Boissière; pp24-29 all images, except p26, courtesy of the Science Photo Library; p24 David Parker; p26 courtesy of the Derby Museum and Art Gallery; p27 (above) Francis Leroy, (below) Adam Hart-Davis; p28 Philippe Plailly; p29 Dr Gene Feldman; p30 Mario Bettella; p34 courtesy of Warner Bros Studios; p39 courtesy of the Shimizu Corporation; pp48-50, p54 Eamonn O'Mahony; p53 Andrew Wright; pp56 (main image and 2nd, 3rd and 4th insets), p59 Dennis Gilbert; p56 (1st inset) Timothy Soar; pp60-62, 78 Richard Davies; pp64-72 all images courtesy of Professor von Gerkan; p64 (main image, 1st and 4th insets), p68 (2nd and 3rd insets) Richard Bryant; p68 (2nd and 3rd insets) Wolf-Deiter Gericke; pp68 (bottom image), p71 Heiner Leiska; p68 (1st inset) Michael Wortman; back cover and pp72-77 Paolo Rosselli; p82 Geoff Beeckman (main image and 1st inset); p84 Dan Cornish; p92 (main image) Tomio Ohashi, (1st and 2nd insets) Yasufumi Kijima; inside covers and pp94-96 Mitsumasa Fujitsuka

CONSULTANTS: Catherine Cooke, Terry Farrell, Kenneth Frampton, Charles Jencks
Heinrich Klotz, Leon Krier, Robert Maxwell, Demetri Porphyrios, Kenneth Powell, Colin Rowe, Derek Walker

HOUSE EDITOR: Maggie Toy EDITORIAL TEAM: Nicola Hodges, Ramona Khambatta, Katherine MacInnes
SENIOR DESIGNER: Andrea Bettella DESIGN CO-ORDINATOR: Mario Bettella
DESIGN TEAM: Gregory Mills, Owen Thomas, Jacqueline Grosvenor

First published in Great Britain in 1993 by *Architectural Design* an imprint of
ACADEMY GROUP LTD, 42 LEINSTER GARDENS, LONDON W2 3AN
Members of the VCH Publishing Group
ISBN: 1-85490-197-4 (UK)

Copyright © 1993 the Academy Group Ltd *All rights reserved*
The entire contents of this publication are copyright and cannot be reproduced
in any manner whatsoever without written permission from the publishers

The Publishers and Editor do not hold themselves responsible for the opinions expressed by the
writers of articles or letters in this magazine
Copyright of articles and illustrations may belong to individual writers or artists
Architectural Design Profile 104 is published as part of *Architectural Design* Vol 63 7-8/1993
Architectural Design Magazine is published six times a year and is available by subscription

Distributed in the United States of America by
ST MARTIN'S PRESS, 175 FIFTH AVENUE, NEW YORK, NY 10010

Printed and bound in Singapore

Contents

SANTIAGO CALATRAVA, LYON AIRPORT RAILWAY STATION, VAULTED STRUCTURE

ARCHITECTURAL DESIGN PROFILE No 104

VISIONS FOR THE FUTURE

Maggie Toy Aspects of Utopia 6
Jean Nouvel Tomorrow Can Take Care of Itself 8
Michael Davies Changes in the Rules 20
Guy Battle and Christopher McCarthy Multi-Source Synthesis 24
Hans Helms The City Shaken 30
Maxwell Hutchinson Rethinking the Future 34
Michael Spens The National Writing Centre and City Library, Swansea 40
Alsop & Störmer Ty Llen, Swansea 44
Richard Rogers Partnership Inland Revenue Headquarters, Nottingham 48
Tomigaya II, Tokyo 52
Lu Jia Zui, Shanghai 54
Norman Foster and Partners Cranfield Library, Bedfordshire 56
Duisburg Micro Electronics Park, Neudorf 60
Von Gerkan, Marg and Partners Passenger Terminal, Stuttgart Airport 64
City Rail Stop, Bielefeld 68
Sony Berlin GMBH 70
Santiago Calatrava Lyon Airport Railway Station 72
Future Systems Green Building, London 78
Visitors' Centre Stonehenge, Salisbury 82
Peter Pran of Ellerbe Becket and Michael Fieldman New York Police Academy 84
Hajime Yatsuka Ni-igata Civic Centre 88
Nasunogahara Harmony Hall 90
Yasufumi Kijima A-B Concept Model 92
Kiko Mozuna Notojima Glass Art Museum 94

MAGGIE TOY
ASPECTS OF UTOPIA

Architecture, from the earliest times, has had two purposes: on the one hand, the purely utilitarian one of affording warmth and shelter; on the other, the political one of impressing an idea upon mankind by means of the splendour of its expression in stone. Bertrand Russell

Although Bertrand Russell's elegant simplification, if interpreted freely, can still be applied today, it is drastically in need of updating. With the advances made in modern technology, it becomes possible to create a building which gives shelter more efficiently than ever; one which not only gives warmth but can afford the comfort of cool air should this be necessary, and so on. In fulfilling this aspect of its purpose, architecture also throws open and wide the possibilities of a structure which can communicate an impressive view to its audience in a spectacular way. However, today the practice falls behind other fields which are experimenting and utilising these advances. This stands in contrast to the best architecture of previous ages that extended the boundaries within which it was set. Consider the gothic master builders who, concerned with the quality of light and the atmosphere within their cathedrals, tested materials to the limit and frequently to the point of failure, in order to ensure that the best effect possible would be created. Likewise, the engineer Auguste Perret, who early this century, used the materials available to him and put them to unprecedented, rigorous tests in order to create an architecture that was both functional and stunning. Examples of this nature are never-ending.

We have more technology available to us than ever before. Should we not be using this ever-increasing knowledge to advance our architecture and to design with this in mind? In addition to this, we must respond to the increasing need to work with a more realistic and sensitive view of the imminent breakdown of the ecological system. Fortunately there are designers who are working towards this goal and this issue explores several varied approaches to the challenge.

Jean Nouvel discusses his work and his view of tomorrow, which, in his opinion, we cannot and therefore should not predict. But many of his schemes, including his *Tour Sans Fins*, communicate an exciting prediction of future possibilities available with expert engineering. Michael Davies from the Richard Rogers Partnership explains the history of technological development and discusses the ecological approach held by the firm. Their schemes illustrate a consistent awareness of the importance of designing in favour of the eco-system, and reveal the extent to which they detail projects in such a way as to make the most of available natural forces. Guy Battle and Christopher McCarthy – engineers who have recently formed a new partnership after many years with Arups and have worked with many of the teams of architects featured in this issue – convey the excitement for future possibilities in architecture by extracting potential examples of progress in other industries which could be interpreted and adopted by architects. These are some examples of transfer technology.

A fatalistic economic point of view is expressed by Hans Helms and presents a necessary contrast to the other positive and exciting opinions. Maxwell Hutchinson draws together a series of parallels which illustrate areas of visionary potential. Will Alsop's new concept for a library project in Swansea, recently won by Alsop & Störmer, is described by Michael Spens. This vision of the way libraries should be approached in the future is a project whose realisation will demonstrate an original way of using technology in the improvement of an existing building type.

Many other projects are also included which in their own way contribute a vision for the future. The visual futuristic approach is illustrated both by Norman Foster and Peter Pran; the latter's scheme for the New York Police Academy has been heralded as an innovative approach to such a challenge. Foster's continuing talent for forward thinking architecture is visible in the two projects Cranfield and Duisburg Micro Electronic Park. Meinhard von Gerkan's maxim 'The best is simple' is manifested in his impressive constructions within Germany. He has developed an individual and yet commercially successful approach to the future of architecture, which has led to his practice achieving eighty competitions wins. His original oeuvre is demonstrated in the examples of Stuttgart Airport (with its tree-like supporting columns) and the station at Bielefeld, as well as the unique Sony Building in Berlin.

The work of the engineer Santiago Calatrava is currently enjoying appropriate exposure. Akin to Perret, currently available materials are tested until they reach their potential; leaving us with wonderful sights such as the Airport Railway station at Lyon. Although of innovative character in its present form, this building will assume even greater futuristic impact once it is finished. Uncompromising in their pursuit of architectural perfection is the Future Systems team: Amanda Levette and Jan Kaplicky. Their Green Building exemplifies the opportunities available to create an architecture that is environmentally friendly and sets an example for individual interpretation. A keen ideology pervades the overall design and extends down to the finest detail. No thoughts that dwell on the future of architecture would be complete without reference to various Japanese projects. The work of Hajime Yatsuka, Yasufumi Kijima and Kiko Mozuna demonstrates the Japanese freedom of thought within architecture and their enthusiasm for experimentation. Their work is indicative of how a particular nation can actually foster an unshackled architectural vision.

Humanity's deepest desire for knowledge drives our continuing quest to extend the limits of architecture, perfecting its nature to suit the purpose in searching for the ultimate in architecture, the ultimate shelter and the ultimate political statement. This condition can, by definition, never be reached as it reveals ever-shifting parameters, but each achievement along the way can enthuse us, inspire awe and stimulate the desire to advance and improve.

OPPOSITE: Jean Nouvel, Tour Sans Fins

JEAN NOUVEL IN CONVERSATION
TOMORROW CAN TAKE CARE OF ITSELF

Few architects have been eager to play the role of committed intellectual in today's cultural debate. The high quality of Nouvel's discourse makes it a part of a cultural debate that is above the level usually found in a highly specialised discipline like architecture. One of the subjects that Nouvel has repeatedly discussed is the supposed immaterialisation of architecture. That process, in his view, would not stop at Modernist achievements such as screen facades and structural steelwork but has continued through to the level of the meaning of the building itself, which eventually becomes merely a climate-regulating shell around autonomous internal processes. The front, once thought of as the boundary of the architectural object, is reduced to an interface between different modes of existence. There is no longer any inside and outside; in fact all the previous functions of the front have ceased to exist. We are in a permanent state of transition and the interface will limit any interruption in this flux to a minimum. In addition to his defence of this approach to the profession, Nouvel has become involved in the discussion concerning the problem of the specialist in a culture that is undergoing the virtualisation of reality through modern technological media such as television, video, fax machines, modems, etc, which lead to space and time shrinking till they eventually merge in an ultimate simultaneity. This development has enormous implications for architecture that has traditionally been understood as being the bringing together of space and materials in the context of time. In order to establish its position in this process it will have to give an explicit account of itself. A simple rejection is not the correct answer in Nouvel's view. This time of 'afterwards' demands a more subtle attitude. It is still a matter of thinking in stone. Architects are in a sense responsible for the environment and Nouvel regards his task as that of doing justice to the new character of our experience of the environment. He lays as little stress as possible on the physical transition between inside and outside, between public and private. Entirely in keeping with the relativising of every hierarchy, you never know precisely where you are as you follow your route through the building; nor, from an institutional point of view, do you know what you are. You are caught up in Nouvel's circulation. In the end you come up against the problem of identity: in this virtual reality you no longer know who you are. With his increased emphasis on practice, Nouvel has opted for a reconquest of innocence. His aim is to heal the Cartesian fissure. The dichotomy between subject and world, between words and things, a divide that modern French philosophers have presented with some emphasis as being unavoidable, can only be overcome by the existential act of life dirtying its own hands. The hyperconscious Nouvel would be only too pleased to lose some of his understanding of life.

If one leafs through any article about contemporary architecture, or goes to any symposium on the subject, the name Jean Nouvel is bound to crop up. How do you feel about that?

That's not my problem, though of course you function better when you know that a majority of people approve of what you're doing. I can't complain about that. People's reactions are fairly predictable: in the first phase the word provocation comes up. People don't understand what I am doing and accuse me of seeking a confrontation. Then there is a phase where I have to explain things to important discussion partners such as clients, administrators and politicians. Once the work of construction is completed you get another set of heated reactions; but the building hopefully will be its own best advocate.

I am certainly not looking for everyone's approval. My architecture is committed in the sense that it argues for a certain attitude towards the present. I expect to get reactions to this attitude: ideological ones and more directly sensory responses; I don't have any problem with them because the majority of them are favourable. The worst thing would be if there were no reactions at all. But I am not trying to elicit them; there is no sense in which I organise or orchestrate them. They usually come of their own accord – that's something I can feel satisfied about.

Who goes to make up your public?

Everyone, but above all the users, the people for instance who in the general way of things make use of the Institut du Monde Arabe or the Institut National de la Recherche Scientifique as visitors or to work in these institutions. You don't choose a public like this; it is a *fait accompli*. Lovers of architecture form an additional public, but they are of secondary importance. Depending on the purpose of the building, there is bound to be a public. Everything else is secondary.

OPPOSITE: IMA (Institut du Monde Arabe), Paris; INSET, ABOVE TO BELOW: Galeries Lafayette, Berlin, (x3); Opéra de Tokyo, Japan

9

One of the most important themes of your writings, your interviews and, for that matter, your buildings is the need for architecture to be 'up to date', to keep abreast, that is, of current cultural developments. Why do you give this quality such priority?

Because I think that architecture is not an autonomous discipline and that it is bound to reflect the culture of a period. It is the visible evidence of its own time and of the preoccupations and aspirations of its own generation. We can never do much more than bear witness to everything that stimulates, excites and gives pleasure to our own generation. I often think that we wouldn't understand anything about the Greeks or the Middle Ages if we didn't have their buildings. That is why I always try to keep up with what is going on; not from day to day as in fashion, nor in terms of decades that the notion of 'design' seems so dependent on, but in the sense of responding to all the aesthetic and emotional values of a given moment.

But that also means that you have to be able to give a diagnosis of a period or a situation?

Yes, that's true; it means one must have a capacity for synthesis; you need both to be aware of what's going on and to be able to distance yourself. An architect, like a film-maker, should know how to take the correct distance, to survey the whole and be able to analyse the details. But isn't this true of all kinds of activity? What does a good rugby or soccer player do if not place himself above the field in order to survey the situation?

The difference is that you don't just survey the situation, you also offer a pathology. Your work contains a certain view of historical destiny, a mixture of fantasy and apocalyptic elements.

The greatest difficulty is always first and foremost how you deal with historical destiny. There are certain facts that you can't get around, such as your historical and geographical circumstances. These are things that neither the will of a single person nor a local political decision can ignore. In our time, for instance, there is no longer any point in grumbling about the environmental chaos caused by the explosive growth of so many cities and suburbs. What's the point of complaining? That's just how things are. Nobody is going to pull everything down and erect, say, an 18th-century city all over again. What I'm interested in is to try and see something positive in what is happening at the moment. Being an architect means choosing to be realistic; otherwise you're not an architect at all. At best you can make nice designs for abstractions such as Human Beings and Ideal Space. They may even be very beautiful, but being an architect means that you have to be capable of building something in a given situation at a given point in time; you must be prepared to do this in the world that is what it is, with all its political, financial and technological limitations.

That's always been my aim. When I see what is going on today, I tell myself: I have to make sure I'm operating in this context and that I'm making something that gives a meaning to that context. That is much more important than the building in itself. An architecture that genuinely deserves to be called interesting always reveals the context; letting it be seen, rather than exploiting it so it appears more important. This is a greater achievement than designing something that is in itself good but which completely ignores its surroundings. Once again, I believe that the philosophy of architecture is a constructive and realistic one. As architects, it is our job to make the world more liveable; a little more lucid and beautiful than it was before. This means *practice*.

Do you think that people can become more free as a result of their architectural surroundings; is there an architecture that can enable us to think more clearly?

It's my conviction that the only really worthwhile gift you can give anyone is the joy and pleasure that you communicate. If someone feels good in a building and thinks it is beautiful and wants to stay there or return to it and talks about it with his friends, then something is going on that is of real importance, something that can change people's experiences and ideas. One can speak of architecture as being real if by means of something tangible something is influenced in the mental realm. I remain convinced that you can distinguish a true architect from a false one as easily as anything: the true one is the one whose finished project is always more interesting than his drawings and maquettes. With the false one the reverse is true. He lets himself be carried away at the drawing board by all kinds of bright ideas, ideas that vanish as quickly as they appeared or else they fall flat as soon as they are tested against reality. A good building is always a hundred times more interesting than the photos and drawings.

If you talk about architecture having the power to change people's experiences and ideas, that suggests you are very optimistic?

In eternity, all we are is little atoms and an architect's buildings only last a little bit longer than we do. In my view, the only hope an architect can have is to make something permanent out of a set of emotions that belong to a very short-lived moment. The capacity for capturing or freezing the values concealed in a specific moment, that is the power of architecture.

I love the fragility you get when something extremely fleeting is petrified. That is why I always work very hard at the different varieties of light in which my work can be seen: by daylight, in the

Hôtel Saint James, Bordeaux

evening, when it is raining or when the sun is shining, from a distance and close to, etc. Architecture for me is not a sort of cold geometrical object that you only allow to affect your reason. The way you experience a building in these different situations is far more important. A building changes according to the weather. In Chartres, when a ray of sunlight falls right through the arched windows or the rose window, the cathedral becomes ten times more alive. It's so simple: buildings are intended for certain moments, like the signs in a musical composition. Certain places were designed for certain events. Churches, for instance, are for spectacle, for theatre and choral singing. Every building should be the ideal place for some people in some situations at some moments in time. This is the fundamental nature of architecture that has any quality.

The striking thing about what you are saying is the opposition between this direct sensation, linked to a specific moment, and the deeper intelligent analysis of a society and of an age which needs to produce architectural forms. Which of these considerations comes first with you?

This opposition is no secret. In my work I am an advocate of making use of every opportunity and every pretext. This means that I don't believe in any generalisation, especially if it is a political one. Of course there is a larger context, but even so what you basically have to do is to forget every notion of a model to be followed, every trace of a conformist attitude. In my view this goes not just for architecture but for every profession, even politics. It is my view that we often have to prise ourselves loose from so-called political necessities. Fate is something that is over and above politics. Sometimes it can seem for a while as though it is political in character, but there are much stronger, more ineluctable bonds such as one's historical inheritance, technological development etc, that weigh more. It isn't the architecture that makes a new world. Godard once said that he didn't have any idea of making a good film; he just wanted to make a film. This means that there is a moment when you just have to practise your profession and you cannot let all kinds of other considerations get in the way of it.

Isn't that being a bit naive?

Again it isn't a question of naivety but of fate. At a certain moment you get into a situation where you need some kind of general perspective in order to know that right here and now there is only one thing that you can do. In any case the idea that you might be able to change the world with a film, a building etc, is pretty ridiculous. You have to be aware of how much influence you have and above all what its limits are.

Isn't there such a thing as being too aware?

No, that's never a disadavantage. You always need to have as much awareness as possible. What is a mistake is to expect too much because you have too optimistic an estimate of the situation: yes, that's something that can have serious consequences, because it leads to being ridiculous, to pretentiousness, to something that no longer has anything to do with architecture. I repeat, the architect has a very simple problem. Nothing that I build is equal to how I imagined it, I'd be the first to admit that. As soon as I start, I put one foot carefully in front of the other till suddenly I feel the ground fall away. With one leg I'm still standing on solid ground. It's when you're in this position, with one foot on the ground and the other in empty space, that you're being a good architect. Sometimes you put both feet in space; that means the building won't be built. You fall flat on your face. A fiasco like that means your idea was too radical, too subversive, incomprehensible. Architecture continues to be the art form that depends on the greatest possible consensus. Perhaps the same goes for films. But compare this with a writer, a painter, a photographer. They do what they like! If we do what we like, we make a little drawing on a piece of paper, but that isn't architecture. In the same way a filmaker can dash off a scenario but that doesn't mean he's made a film!

So far we have looked at your métier from the point of view of the artist. Can you also describe it from the institutional point of view of the commission that has to be realised?

The least you can expect from an architect who has his head screwed on is that he will respect the commission. Architecture has suffered a lot from things being produced that went right against any kind of reality, that had nothing to do with the world as it actually exists, as we experience it everyday. I don't think it's an insurmountable problem if some buildings have elements that don't quite make sense, for instance, with regard to their upkeep. But they have to make sense for the people who have to live in them. I pay a great deal of attention to this. As far as participation is concerned I am an heir of May 68. The questions raised by the assignment should be discussed democratically. On the other hand I don't believe in creativity by referendum. That doesn't work.

You have given a full description of your personal approach to architecture. What do you think however, about the possibility of achieving an ecological and social balance?

I hardly need to tell you that we live in a situation of balances that are constantly being upset. This is called dynamics. I don't have any belief whatsoever in restoring the balance by going back in time. What

Hôtel Saint James, Bordeaux

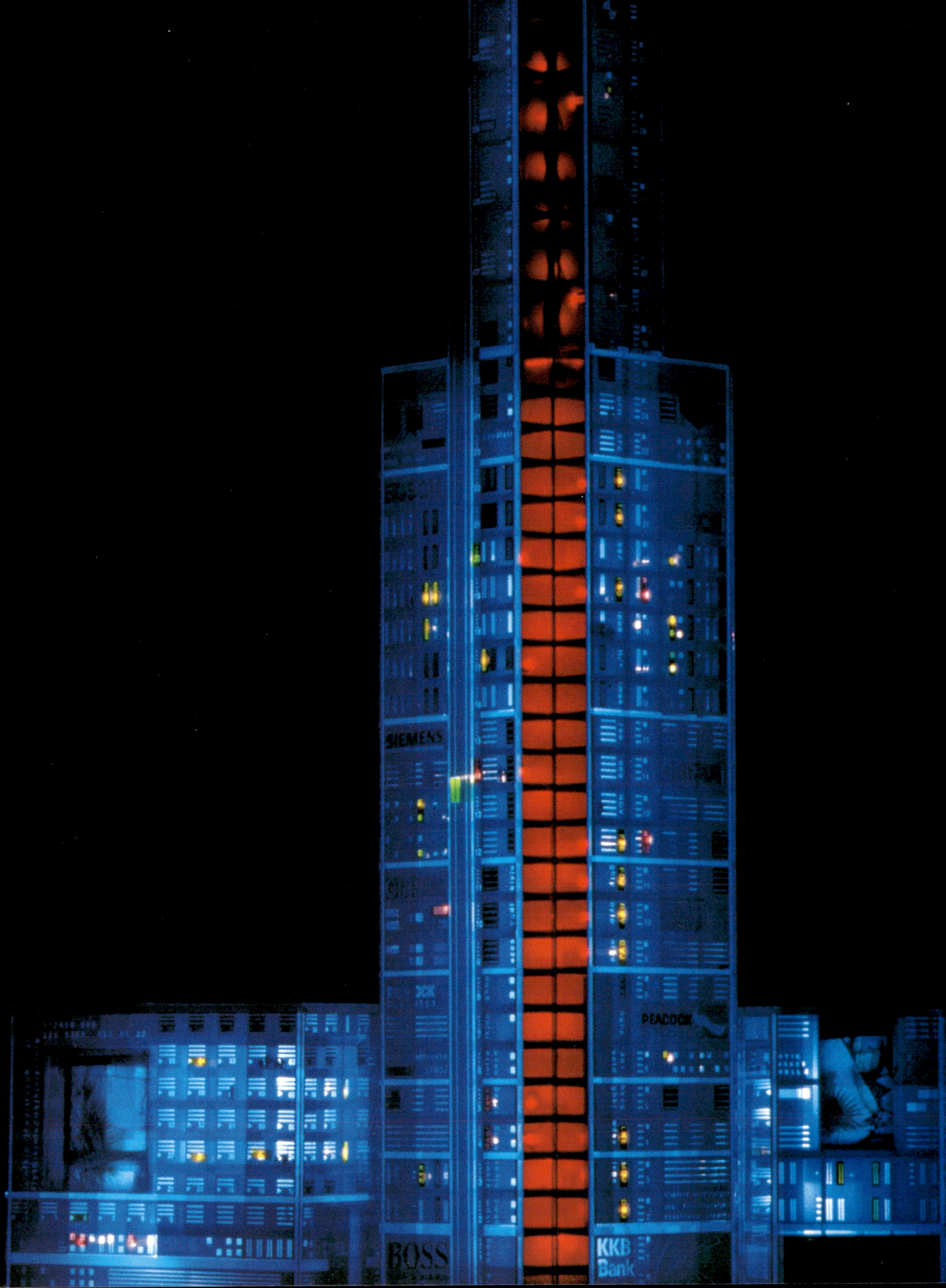

I do believe in is a permanent lack of balance while we search for something that lies ahead of us; as long as we put one foot in front of the other and don't fall flat on our faces. What's more, I am not particularly interested in all these ideologies that appear on the stage one after the other; the present ecological ideology, for instance, 3/4 of which consists of a somewhat suspect nostalgia. I have great faith in the future, but not in the sense of having unlimited time at your disposal or as a system of predictions. I never allow myself to forget that I am not building for tomorrow, but for today; even though I would love to live 5,000 years later. That's just my nostalgia for the future. I have already been talking for 15 years about dematerialisation in architecture. This also has to do with the development of new technologies, and the circumstances in which architects work. Right from the start people have tried to build as lightly and as simply as possible to shelter themselves against wind, cold and rain.

Seeing that gravity exists whether we like it or not, the architect's job is always to use the means at his disposal to make a structure that is as satisfying as possible, both in the relation between inside and outside and in terms of light. At one moment people want everything lit up and the next they want no light from outside to enter in. You can't have it both ways. It's my view that our possibilities have increased considerably this century. At the same time I think that modernity is a living concept whose content is in evolution. And I think that a building where the only idea is to show the structural reality will first and foremost be a boring building. I think that if a structure only invites you to say things like 'Oh, what a beautiful pillar! Oh, what a beautiful beam!', it is saying very little. As far as I am concerned I try to use less obvious means to make buildings that are thought-provoking or emotionally inspiring: symbolism, for instance, or the incidence of light, through their tangibility, how the rooms follow on from each other, the setting. For me these are the terms that belong to today and today's emotions.

But this concern with today's terms surely originates in a historical vision that also takes into account what is implicit in the present and where that is leading us. What's going to happen tomorrow?

In this sense the future is simply a dream about something that we can't possibly know for certain. I don't allow myself to imagine what I will think about my buildings in 30 years time. Time doesn't interest me, only the present moment. Every time people fancied that they were building for the future, they ended up with a flop. The same goes for all those plans for cities and neighbourhoods for 15 or 20 years time. I just said it a moment ago: we would do better to know what our limitations are. I do not think of my buildings as belonging to the future but as being as intelligent as possible and appealing to people's senses and feelings as effectively as is possible *now*. 'Tomorrow' can take care of itself. I can't possibly know what they will discover tomorrow, what wars will take place, what the social developments will be in the neighbourhood for which I am making this building. Its greatest chance of survival will be if I make it as relevant and meaningful as possible for *now*. Then maybe people will allow it to remain as a piece of evidence and they will even feel affection for it. That is all I can do. I have nothing to say about what will come after our time. I am not a clairvoyant; if you want a fortune teller you should go to the fairground.

You predicted that 'the future of architecture will no longer be architectural'.

That's something I'm convinced about. I made nine tenths of all the architects in France furious when I said that – all the professors of architecture, whole schools of them! They think that architecture is buried away somewhere in the genes of the profession, in other words in its whole history. And they think they can guess what the next phase will be because they know the entire history from Babylon to Louis Kahn.

They couldn't be more wrong if they tried! Because the most important factor in the next phase is not the whole history of architecture but everything that is going on in the world at the precise moment when a new architecture is produced. It's fine by me if people know everything about history if they intended to use it, but it isn't the most important thing! What you need to get a grip on is the fact that in our time with its enormous production of images and its technological processes, people are exposed to a bombardment of information. The result of all this is a new notion of the whole visible reality. It should be clear then that the architecture of the future will hardly be influenced at all by what we have now. The thing that interests me is the poetry of a situation and finding a meaning in a context of plurality. I am not someone who loves what is pure to the exclusion of what is impure; I love them both. I love everything.

I make conceptual architecture. Architecture has to be conceptual. In our office we don't make the drawings first; the first two weeks we have discussions and these, of course, take the form of words. If we could say in words what we wanted to make, then the project would in fact already be finished. Do you see what I am getting at?

On the other hand, the piece of architecture may start with words, but the words are the first thing that gets forgotten. What remains is the architecture. The most irritating thing in my view is to talk too much about architecture, because words have a very arbitrary relationship with architecture. You need to forget the words because the architecture will say it with other means. For me words are part of a personal way of working that isn't interesting to

Tour sans Fins, La Défense, Paris (photomontage); OPPOSITE: Media Park, Cologne

anyone and isn't interesting for architecture either. All it is, is the material momentum of my thought processes.

While we are on this subject, what do you think about the heteronymy of the ideas that go to make up the design of a building and the fait accompli *that modern society presents us with? The dissolution of what was intended in the actual result?*

This brings us to a highly philosophical discussion about the historical and economical inevitability of buildings, their affective content and their discourse which can totally be wiped out by events. I think myself that architecture must have, will have to have, a transcendent dimension over and above all that. It will have to be able to adapt to the greatest and most catastrophic changes, even if only in its references. It is a good thing if you can picture your building as it would be in a situation of neglect or mutilation, of violence being done to it, of an extreme alienation from its goal. Buildings to which the most terrible things have happened can be just as astonishing and emotionally charged as an architecture that has always been perfectly maintained and cared for. We have to accept the whole paradoxical relation between the partially unfulfilled aspirations of a building and what actually happens to it in reality.

Like a singer who never knows precisely how his voice sounds?

Yes, that's it; it's the relation between what is intended and the actual result, the proportion of what was not achieved to the element that was fundamental. Is that all you can do, taking small steps or avoiding risks? Architecture is in any case so much a form of applied art that for that reason, if for none other, you cannot avoid the necessity of costing your building according to social and functional requirements. And with these requirements all kinds of other aims and messages creep in, some of them recognised but others that are often hidden. But there are also elements in the design that the architect can turn at his own discretion into a hidden sign or message that can only be decoded by his equals. The architect's own ideas may be shocking or subversive, as long as they are not expressed openly. The architect writes a sort of text consisting of different levels; the most personal of these can only be read between the lines.

If you look at the filmic quality of architecture, what sort of film do you think of?

I see the contemporary film director as a sort of architect. He has to put forward a draft plan that may or may not be accepted. There are administrative, financial, technical and organisational considerations. In a short period of time he has to bring a large team of people together in one place. But there are other similarities as well. In what I call the architectural substratum we experience the influence on time and space of the filmic aspect. The camera moves through a series of tableaus, puts a frame round the action, sheds various sorts of light on it. All this helps me in designing a building, when I am thinking of how one enters it and moves from one room to another, the meetings that take place and how one leaves it. This 'scenography' of the building is more than just the decor; it is a sort of play in itself. Take the IMA, for instance, for me this was a design based entirely on the idea of movement *forward*. As far as the 'editing' of the textures is concerned, if it isn't film, it is in any case video. In this respect architecture stands at the crossroads of a whole variety of influences.

By using the currently popular baroque means of architecture, you would seem to want to comment on the institutional aspect of the relation between design and programme; for instance, in the Media Park in Cologne.

The Media Park is reasonably accessible as a project and can definitely not be described as heroic. It was actually a 'faster' project than most of the other projects I have worked on. The aim was to conceive a programme that would be just as readable by night as by day. This was possible with the aid of various devices, amongst them the Potemkin screen, but with holes in them.
Broadly speaking, the idea of a programmed building that you can see the life going on in and in which the typical images give you a clue as to what the whole building is like, this idea is typical of the average business quarter at the present day. The difference in my case is that I work a little faster than those people who all pay more attention to their 'image'. The Media Park is more a way of crystallising those aesthetic experiences that are connected with reading a computer screen; these can be beautiful without, for instance, it being possible to take photos of them. It is a question then of recreating a completely different scale, an aspect of architecture that is extremely illuminating and dynamic and that corresponds to one of the typical visual pleasures of today's world. That is why it is a good thing to design something of that sort. They are projects that employ a number of means that are not yet very popular but which can profoundly affect the poetry of the city. If there are many buildings of this sort in a single street then they would after a while have a somewhat disturbing effect. That is obvious enough. But if the whole city was like that, then of course the character of the city itself would change and so, in the long term, would one's perception of what a city is.

That means that if your work is repeated often enough it can have a profound influence on one's

OPPOSITE: Galeries Lafayette; OVERLEAF: Residence Cap D'Ail, France; INSET, ABOVE TO BELOW: Residence Cap D'Ail, France; Hôtel Saint James, Bordeaux; Nemausus, Nîmes

perceptual equipment. What is left then of that uncritical fascination with fate? Is there anything left that is lasting?

What I've just been describing is an important element in my work but not the only one. The blueprint for the Tour sans Fins in La Défense, for example, is a another kind altogether. There you can find more lasting and metaphysical aspects and not just the element of fragility that I mentioned earlier on. But in my architecture the idea of something lasting is not expressed by the form but by the mentality. That's what it's all about. You see, I am very fond of buildings that reveal their fragility and their makeshift character. The thing that preoccupies me is that all buildings can actually be protected only in one way. Not by using granite or reinforced concrete; something like that will at most make a difference of a few years. It is not a matter of civilisation surviving. A building must above all be a step in the architectural history of a specific moment of civilisation. Only then will it represent something; only then can people feel love for it and that is the basic requirement for permanence. The Katsura architecture in Japan, or the Eiffel Tower remain standing – however unstable buildings like that are – because people love them. It is not really important for the walls to be a metre thick. One can of course think up other formulas for success; all I can say is that they're not mine.

What I mean by this is that the more institutional a building is, the more it embodies something that has to do with the culture, the more it will have an aesthetic value; and whatever the structural state of a building like that, it will be preserved. It should also be fairly obvious that things like that no longer have anything to do with architecture as such.

With an approach like that you disqualify a great number of your colleagues who give priority to autonomous professionalism. You must have many enemies.

That's true. In France, if you aren't a historicist, or a neo-modernist and if you're not a supporter of architecture as an autonomous academic discipline, then you already have two-thirds of the nation against you. Isn't it strange, however, that an architect who passes for a notorious eclectic, who always reacts to the specific context, has so many enemies. You might think that such an eclectic would be everybody's friend but the opposite proves to be the case. Because I have no intention of ever building a historicising or purely modernist building, my architectural handwriting will never easily be accepted by a large group of people, no matter how carefully I respond to the specific character of a site. You see, people are fondest of things that reoccur all the time. Just think how many followers people have who always make the same things; it is not a coincidence that they get the opportunity to do just that. With my work people generally feel a little ill at ease because in each case they feel forced to adopt a different attitude.

If we apply to your concrete work this question of the difficulty people experience in accepting what you do, the aspect of boundaries or limits is perhaps a good way to begin. It is in fact there that you get the possibility of breaking through the standard patterns of historicism and modernism with their all too familiar physical framework.

It is a matter of how you land in a certain situation. As far as I am concerned I think the most interesting thing is if someone can end up somewhere without having to make a whole series of moves first. Academic architecture always lets you know that you are approaching something somewhere a kilometre in advance. And, sure enough, in the end you do end up somewhere. As for myself I'd like to be inside somewhere immediately. This also brings us to the notion of an interface; all one has to do is to go through a screen. The boundary has become virtual and that also has something to do with being tactile. My plan for a Tour sans Fins in La Défense has something to do with that, but only lengthwise. The project on the Boulevard Raspail is another case in point. You simply cannot tell where the building begins and where it ends; you can see the sky through it. Inside you see trees growing. It is difficult to decide which is the real entrance because you enter the building at least three or four times. At one time you go through the screens; then you pass through an eight-metre high glass door. Meanwhile, you still think you are outside. And suddenly you are in the lift; once again this is made of glass. You don't even know that you are in a lift, until it starts to move. What I mean to say by this is that the whole problem of boundaries is actually first and foremost a problem of interference. It is a question of the deeper meaning of a building or a space, of the whole way in which one perceives the structure and routes, that with the help of the interface, can be eliminated. This means that the boundary becomes increasingly virtual. In many of my projects you enter from below like a spaceship. The door in the sense of a door-tool is physically eliminated. You take an escalator and suddenly disappear. There is no more door, only flowing movements.

There is yet another dimension that is important and that is ubiquity, being everywhere at once; this has to do with the wonder one feels for the faculty of perception as a function of speed. In the project in Nogent sur Marne for a nightclub, this is very relevant because an extensive video system has been installed there. Inside and outside are simultaneously present; what is more, our eyes see both the reality and the film. In the end you no longer know where you are. The space has become virtual because all that one sees is in fact a space which people imagine they have made their own. It is still of course a matter of the layout of the terrain and the interconnections, but no longer of the space in the mathematical sense of the word. Or rather, the whole aesthetic system of the building is a system that exists outside the boundary.

Then, of course, there is the question of how the building is seen from outside, from a car or a plane, by daytime or at night. And if one thinks about these matters of perception, one will have to admit that the meaning of architecture changes. These are questions that have everything to do with present cultural and technological developments. I do not relate to the idea of an actual apocalypse, but I am definitely fascinated by visions like that of Baudrillard about the fatality of things empowering us. That's also why, despite all attempts at devising a context and a programme, I think that you still have to hold on to the autonomous power of something that continues to make sense, even in a situation where the context is totally subverted so that the opposite happens from what one had planned. This field of tension can be seen very clearly in the Institut du Monde Arabe, where because of a lack of financial resources the building hasn't been cleaned for four years, even though a million visitors have passed through it. I could never have dreamed of something like that. The thing that is so interesting about this is that despite all the objective evidence of decay, the building continues to have dignity.

Isn't it actually much more interesting to speculate on the field of tension between your own cultural relativism on the one hand and Arab absolutism on the other, that still apparently manage to be reconciled in your architecture? If architecture wishes to participate in the cultural debate, this sort of tension is a rewarding theme, because it is something like this that enables us to see that architecture belongs within the realm of culture and not outside it. What is more, when you look at it from the architect's point of view, he or she is also just another ordinary citizen and as such, is a potential participant in the democratic discussion about the options: the possibilities and the specific needs of our society.

No, as an architect I can't answer that. As an architect you can't carry the problems of the human race, or all the international problems on your own shoulders. Of course, as an ordinary citizen I'll be only too pleased to talk about these things at the bar of the Café de Commerce, but as an architect that's not my problem. Political questions like racism and integration, economic and financial matters, in as much as they have any relevance to my work, are more than I can be expected to cope with. And that's just as well. We are only just beginning to put the period behind us when we were all traumatised by architects who wanted to explain the world and to lay down sets of rules for achieving Utopia. I'm for architects having a completely different role. Every cultural attitude is potentially a critical one, although I believe that there have been times when that made more sense than it does in our time. At present, in my opinion it's a question first and foremost of the *hope* that the political attitude essentially implied. I mean hope in a broad sense and not in the sense of some notion of progress. I've got nothing against a situation where a number of architects get involved directly with politics out of a desire for change. I am also delighted when more people come up with a principled attitude to their city or to architecture that invests them with a certain authority to influence decisions. It's also a good thing when architecture gives voice to its own point of view from its privileged position as a social intersection of interests. All that is well and good. But when all is said and done, your influence as an architect lies in the power of your proposals and your designs. Or even in a statement that is in some sense poetic in character. When a building has actually been erected and is provocative through the simple fact that it continues to remain standing, it begins to engage in a form of criticism that is much more effective than any story on paper. There is a power in reality and people realise this all too little. The architects who have the most to tell are the ones who actually build.

Excerpt from The Invisible in Architecture, *edited by Ole Bouman and Roemer van Toorn, to be published by Academy Editions in 1994.*

Concept model of Opéra de Tokyo, Japan

MICHAEL DAVIES
CHANGES IN THE RULES

The Egyptians looked at the sky 4,000 years ago and wondered how it worked. They developed a cosmology, an understanding of the universe, in which they suggested that the great arch of the sky was the goddess Knut whose body was covered with diamonds; she swallowed the sun in the evenings and gave birth to the sun in the mornings. Their system explained the universe: the day and night cycle and the stars. For thousands of years that concept was sustained, before being substituted gradually by more scientific thought through the Greek eras and the Middle Ages. With the invention of precision scientific instruments, the universe began to be understood more definitely. The purpose of some of the earliest of these instruments was to measure fairly accurately the positions of the stars in the sky and the movement of the planets. In doing so, the simple ideas and previous cosmologies were revealed to be false and the comfortable concepts of earlier days came under threat.

In 1543 Nicholas Copernicus published *De Revolutionibus,* an astronomical treatise suggesting a sun-centred universe and an earth that moved. It was a theory for which no proof existed. In 1610 Galileo Galilei constructed one of the earliest astronomical telescopes. It caused a huge conceptual and technological shift that completely changed the nature and the way we perceived the universe. This little telescope with its four-centimetre aperture, enabled him to see the satellites of Jupiter and the phases of Venus. Galileo proved that the Earth moved and effectively verified Copernicus' new cosmology which placed the sun at the centre of our solar system around which all the planets rotated. He was arrested and put in prison – people with radical ideas were often suppressed by the authorities of the day because they challenged the status quo. Nevertheless, that sun-centred cosmology superseded the former, reflecting a huge conceptual shift from one system to another – a change in the rules brought about by new technology.

In music, we have been playing traditional instruments for hundreds of years. Researchers in the Institute for Research and Co-ordination in Acoustics and Music in Paris, began in the 70s to study what was popularly known then as computer music. One of the things they did with computers and synthesizers was to try and describe and reproduce the nature of the sound of traditional instruments; for example, why does a violin sound like a violin or a trombone sound like a trombone? Researchers programmed the sounds into the machine and then tried to write programmes which would reproduce these sounds. They reached the point where computer-sound synthesizers were able to reproduce quite convincing sounds such as an oboe, a violin or a trumpet; so the computers began to be able to produce the traditional noises. They also compared the differing sound properties of the violin and trumpet, and programmes which would translate the sound from one instrument into the sound of the other. If the computer started by playing the sound of the violin, it could transform the sound over time until it became the sound of a trumpet. Researchers then realised that if you stopped the computer programme halfway through, you were able to hear sounds which had never been made or heard before. This was a huge conceptual jump. Commencing with instruments we know – and we have three or four hundred instruments with very specific sorts of sounds – we are now in a situation where the computer has been able to fill in this enormous timbral spectrum that was previously largely blank, and it is able to produce the sound of instruments that do not exist. Therefore, by changing technology we have been able to move into a new realm.

Another example of a technological conceptual jump is the development of the sonic tape. The days of the tape measure are now over, for we are able to measure distance by ultra-sound. One can stand in a large space and measure its height, width and depth by sonic means without physically walking through the space: a completely different concept and technology for a job that was previously done by more traditional means. It entailed a conceptual jump from one technology to another. Technology incorporated in such devices is transforming our everyday life and changing our work methods. It is inevitable that such things will have an impact on our building fabric and cities in the future.

So what has been happening in the building industry? Let us go back in history and look at the window. For thousands of years we have been building traditional masonry constructions: from cliff dwellings of several thousand years ago to the large medieval mega-buildings. The great medieval fortresses are virtually without windows; those that exist, are in the form of tiny openings in an immensely solid, thermally inert building. The building was basically a cave, a protection device.

In the Gothic era, the technology of building

advanced substantially and structurally in terms of glazing. We refined glass fabrication and colouring techniques and created great windows and impressive structures. We built larger and larger structures which were not very high in performance, apart from their structural capability. The great cathedrals were built for the glory of God, not for the comforts of man.

Gradually, technology moved on. By 1675, Europe was incited by the idea of navigation: we were discovering the world. People from all over the world were sailing to other parts. Europe had great fleets of ships which began to trade and to discover. However, in order to do this you had to know where you were and to be aware of the time. You also had to understand the shape of the world, or you would drop off the edge or arrive in the wrong place. In 1675, the Royal observatory was built at Greenwich in London by Christopher Wren. The world's prime meridian zero runs through these buildings. The reason for building the observatory was time and navigation; to understand where you were and to understand location. In doing so, navigators had to look at the stars, for they indicated time and location. A technological building built for technological reasons, the observatory allowed trade around the world to have some form of reference of time and place. Knowing the time and place, changed the rules, and as a result the world changed.

By 1780, the Industrial Revolution had commenced. The greatest structure of the early Industrial Revolution was the iron bridge built at Coalbrookdale by Abraham Darby in 1779. It was the first great cast-iron structure in the world. The bridge had a 30-metre span and was based upon a new understanding of structure, of tension and compression; a conceptual shift where the discovery of cast iron began to open new ground and offer new potentials entirely different from masonry construction. Iron caused a change in the rules.

By the time Le Corbusier was operational, there a sophisticated understanding and use of the new material concrete had evolved. His integration of steel, glass and concrete is displayed magnificently in the Villa Savoie, Poissy, France. The use of glass is very interesting: the whole of the ground floor is really a narrative of glass, of light flooding through from outside to inside, and of transparency and of a feeling of space. This building allows us to appreciate the interplay of three materials steel glass and concrete as a true architectural symphony. Space, form and light are used quite spectacularly. The window onto the terrace of the Villa Savoie was the largest piece of glass in domestic use in Europe at the time (1929). Le Corbusier utilised a small frame at the edge to protect the corner of the glass. However, it was the glass that bore the load; a mobile piece of glass. Le Corbusier was attempting to use a piece of glass as a non-wall: as an absence of wall. The piece of glass winds aside and allows the space to flow through. The architect's inventive spirit is revealed further in his treatment of doors at the Villa Savoie. Usually, a solid door is provided in a solid wall. However here, Le Corbusier left a visual gap: the doors are great clear glass doors in solid walls. The doors are visually open although they are physically closed – another change in the rules. The architect is exploring a different interrelationship between spaces and plays with glass in a very active and consciously architectural way. The Villa Savoie is a wonderful building, although phenomenally cold in the winter and very hot in the summer.

At the same time in 1929, another architect, Pierre Chareau, began to explore with his 'Maison de Verre' in Paris some of the potentials of glass, steel and iron in different ways. Insulative, translucent and transparent panels are woven together in a magnificent interplay of light and shadow, transparency and transience in the facade. Pierre Chareau was attempting to achieve increased performance from his facade, whilst at the same time retaining its lightness transparency, and aesthetic beauty.

In the 30s, Mies van der Rohe came up with an extremist image of the modern skyscraper. The medieval fortress is reversed completely: from a solid masonry building with small windows, we have moved to a skeletal frame clothed entirely in glass. The thesis was: all we have is a wonderfully expressed frame and onto that frame we wrap this amazing transparent 'stone' that will last 500 years. The expression of the architecture is as pure as possible and the idea was wonderfully clear. Of course, nobody ever built it – you would have been able to fry an egg on the floor of the offices! There is an enormous problem of the impact of the external environment on the interior and the huge thermal loss from the internal environment to the exterior.

An attempt to solve the problem of solar gain can be seen with reflective glasses. The Hyatt Hotel in Dallas, built in the early 80s is a fine example of reflective glass technology in a warm climate. The building is a prime example of what has happened to the American wrapper building. Here, mirrors really have been applied all over. The building's transparency and the structural qualities have been lost in the attempt to deal with the solar gain problem. There is quite an interesting structure behind the facade, but it is gone, invisible; and the skin of the building is just a wrapper, like a piece of Christo – brown paper all over the building. Thus, you are paying penalties for defence against the sun, in terms of the other opportunities within the architecture of the building.

We, as architects, were trying to achieve other things with our facades at the same point in time. We wanted to keep transparency, and we have always tried to avoid the problem of the great reflective wrapper where you cannot read the elements of the building. So at the Centre Pompidou building in Paris we consciously avoided using reflective glass and tried to deal with the problem of solar gain by the use of layering. Seven layers of material lie between the glass and the outside of the building.

There are pieces of circulation fabric, there are staircases, there is structure, there are walkways, there are lifts. In some ways it is a sort of *brise-soleil* building. It has that great quality of being able to reverse itself: the building in daytime is completely different from the building at night. In the day, one reads the form and structure and the people flowing through the circulation tubes from the piazza. At night, the building changes completely: you read the guts of the building, you read the interior, you read the transparency, you see the people movement, and you see the great vertical piazza with light streaming out of it.

One of our other projects, the Lloyd's Building in London, incorporates a deliberate attempt to create some secondary interest in the glass itself. The underwriting room of Lloyds is essentially a private market and the public should not be able to see onto the trading floor. With this in mind, we developed a translucent wall that is in fact a triple-skin glass where translucency and a certain sparkle, a certain vitality, were positively sought in the development of the facade. We designed a particular pattern to enliven the glass of the building which gave it a more interesting appearance than the flat sheet. The wall glows in sunlight. Unlike a clear glass wall, it takes on luminous properties similar to those of the great Japanese screens of the past. It also performed a technologically demanding thermal control job in the late 80s energy and information boom. A conscious attempt was made to add a new dimension to the glazing.

Another building which pushes glass into slightly greater performance is the Billingsgate Market in London, which is used as a trading market for financial securities. The market is characterised by visual display units, television screens with their inevitable problems of reflection and glare. We were obliged to develop a glazing system which prevented the sun falling directly onto the screens and which would also keep the luminosity down so that the glare in the room was not unbearable. To solve this problem, we utilised a sophisticated triple-layer glass system with particular properties. We are deliberately making sandwich layers of glass and are beginning to specify different properties in each layer to do a particular sort of job. Here, we custom-designed a mix of layers to try and achieve a particular task: a hint of things to come.

Another problem which affects the facade of a building is the client and his use of the building. The client will occupy the project that you've designed and built and express his thanks for 'a very beautiful building'. However, when you next come back; he has added in new windows to suit his changing needs. You then go back to your office and think: 'What a dreadful client'. But the client is right. It's us architects who are wrong. In the office we call this the 'Reliance Window Syndrome'. The Reliance Control building, was designed in 1965 by Richard Rogers and Norman Foster, who were then partners. It has been modified by the client who said 'I want some more offices, so – bang! – I'll get a saw and I'll cut along the facade and I'll just put a window in'. Of course, he destroyed the visual balance of the building; but why shouldn't he be able to do that? Buildings change their uses over time. Therefore, our practice has been developing buildings which are less precious. We have been deliberately designing things which are more robust: buildings which have got a strong enough facade to survive a client attack. So when the client comes up with his commandos and screws on the air conditioning unit and changes the fire escape, the building does not become an aesthetic wreck.

The PA Technology building in Cambridge is a building where the client said: 'I want a certain percentage of glazing in the building. I don't know where my offices are going to be. I don't know whether they are going to be open plan or closed plan offices. I'm going to shuffle my staff around every three or four months because my staff are project-related, not task-related, and they change with every project. The team size changes, the people change, the secretaries change and the way they work changes.' The building offers great flexibility in terms of use. The facade of the building is really just a patchy set of glazed and solid panels. It is designed as a zipper facade so you can take the panels out and move them around the building to suit different uses. Aesthetically, it is a little bit difficult to handle, but the client is quite happy because he tinkers with it and the architect doesn't come rushing up saying, 'Hey! You can't do that!'

The Lloyd's Building, although essentially built from basic construction materials, attempts to become a dynamically modifiable building; in that its skin, which is the triple layer laminate to which I referred earlier, in fact incorporates the air conditioning of the building. Air is drawn from the interior space through the light-fittings, where it picks up excess energy that we do not want to be introduced into the interior space. This air is then drawn down through the facade itself, between the layers of the glass. The energy, the heat from the room, is then rejected to the exterior if required, or taken away into the heart of the building, processed, and recycled. If it is hot, you can reject energy through the facade. If the building is cool, or a particular piece of the building is cool, you can absorb energy through that facade. In the south facade at Lloyd's you can collect energy in the air circulating in the facade and put it somewhere else in the building. The skin is therefore a crude example of a dynamic control mechanism.

One of the interesting aspects of the Lloyd's Building is that it incorporates an energy-management system which begins to build a network of awareness of the physical fabric of the building. A building energy-management system is essentially a central processing computer which monitors the condition of various parts of the building and its plant. The average aeroplane knows how much fuel there is in the tanks, what the pressure is at the wings, what the ailerons are doing, what the flaps are doing. It is monitoring itself continuously 30 or 40 times a second. The aeroplane knows how it is feeling. I propose that the average building should know how it feels. Such a building is an intelligent building; basically a building which is aware of itself; aware of the energy falling on its facade; aware of the energy coming through the facade; aware of the people inside the building and what their needs are. It is a building which is capable of responding to local energy control and transfer, local glare control and local user tuning in any particular piece of its overall environment. And why shouldn't buildings in the future know if the next morning will be cold or warm and therefore prepare themselves and pre-heat up or pre-cool down? The necessary information is already there and needs only to be made available to the building. If it is a brilliant, sunny day, the south facade of the building darkens down sufficiently to make it comfortable to live in. The concept of the intelligent building, of the intelligent environment, requires a fairly sophisticated, adaptive, dynamically changeable building skin. With Lloyds, we have attempted to integrate the building skin as part of that system. We are now beginning to talk about the concept of the skin of a building as part of its plant and servicing system.

For the first time, switchable facades are available. In our office in Tokyo we have a conference room which is enclosed in clear glass. If you want to have privacy you touch the button and the glass goes white. So you don't pull any blinds, you just press the button and it changes. It is powered by a seven-volt electric current and uses solid state electrochromic materials. The switchable conference room could change the way one thinks about buildings. With the introduction of an electrochromic panel, a truly intelligent facade can be obtained. For the first time, you may have a variable control skin for a building. Here is a device which allows you to adapt the four facades of your buildings differently. You would expect to find the appearance of the east facade different from the south facade and the west facade; and for each to be changing continually. So you may have a building facade which changes from clear to black, to tinted glass, to silver, to pink or blue or any other hue. Our facade is alive and constantly changing like a chameleon skin. We also have our electronic blinds and shutters integrated into the skin of the building.

We are also involved at present in research into what we can do with holographic information in the skin of buildings. Everyone who sees a holographic image sees something different as they are each in different positions. As you move, you see different images. Information may change continuously as you move past it. The building skin is an adaptive three-dimensional information screen.

Our building skin can also power itself. The solar collector of the 60s used to cost £15,000 a square inch. It was built into satellites and used power Gemini spacecraft. Technology began to explore ways of bringing down that cost. We now have solar panels which cost virtually nothing. So we can get energy off the building facade.

For the first time, you can specify the sort of facade you want. You can actually choose the building skin. You can custom design its properties. You can choose the colour; you can let certain frequencies pass through and reflect other frequencies; you can begin to engineer your glass. For the first time you can actually design the skin of the building, like you design everything else. You can specify the properties you want and science is now capable of developing it. The switchable glass, electrochromic glass and holographic materials all exist today, and their costs are dropping towards levels which the building industry can use.

So I see the facade of the future building as an electronic tapestry, a microchemical chameleon. All wiring and cabling, all control engineering is in the facade; including the monitoring logic, the information transfer network and the decision making capacity. The amount of logic required in the average building is really incredibly small. There is no reason why we cannot build the logic, the monitoring devices, the awareness and the response directly into the skin of the building. I would like a building skin where one could change the transparency; where one could dial the insulative properties and change the thermal mass. The technologies are available for a building with a programmable and adaptive facade. It can be multicoloured. It can transmit information. It can process solar energy in and out. It can play tunes for the occupants.

I have talked about the first industrial revolution which made Europe what it is today; which put people on the moon, which saves lives in far-off places with very straightforward and simple medical technology. What has happened in the last ten years is at least as significant as the revolution of 150 years ago. We are now in the middle of the second industrial revolution. We have moved from the valve to the computer. We have moved from the mechanical age to that of the solid state. The world of the 21st century is the solid state world, an enormous conceptual shift yet another change in the rules. An enormous revolution has happened which has changed the world and its potential. Our built environment will be affected by this revolution and we must be prepared to take positive advantage of the new technologies for the improvements of our buildings, our environment and our lifestyle.

'Look up at a spectrum-washed envelope whose surface is a map of its instantaneous performance, stealing energy from the air with an iridescent shrug, ripping its photogrids as a cloud runs across the sun, a wall which as the night chill falls, fluffs up its feathers and turning white on its north face and blue on the south, closes its eyes but not without remembering to pump a little glow down to the night porter, clear a view patch for the lovers on the south side of level 22 and to turn 12 per cent silver just before dawn.'

GUY BATTLE AND CHRISTOPHER McCARTHY
MULTI-SOURCE SYNTHESIS
A Future Engineering Response to Climatic Forces in Architecture

One of the most important things one human can give another is a vision of the future

A primary objective of our profession is to generate comfortable, safe, creative and economic internal and external spaces for people to occupy; buildings designed by people for people. Further to servicing buildings as a means of achieving human environmental satisfaction, architects and engineers are developing building envelopes which will interact with and moderate the adverse effects of the climate, while simultaneously capitalising on free energy resources such as the sun and the wind. Thus, like a cold blooded reptile which raises its scales to the sun to warm itself, our future buildings will respond to climatic change.

Lessons from Nature
The environment within which we live is an ever changing one. Throughout evolution the living world around us has adapted to cope with this varying climate. While the oak tree sways in the wind, the sentry remains still through minute muscular response. Furred animals, such as the polar bear, vary the thickness of the fatty layer and the density of the fur coat that surrounds their bodies. Likewise, some lizards can increase or decrease the area of skin exposed to the sun, and some can vary their own skin colour from light to dark to either reflect or absorb heat more efficiently. In a similar manner, our own human bodies are precise thermoregulators. Our skin is the boundary between our internal organs and the external environment. It manages through a number of mechanisms, such as vasodilation, vasconstruction, sweating and body hair movement, to maintain an almost constant body temperature of 36.8°C.

However, like all animals we choose to moderate the diverse effects of the climate by surrounding ourselves with an enclosure to distance ourselves from our natural environment. Over the centuries we have progressed from the heavy-weight rock cave, to the light-weight glass tower block in an effort to find the most aesthetic, efficient, and comfortable living and working conditions.

Our response has been single minded, to keep the weather out or, in other words, 'environment rejecting'. In climates where there is much high density solar radiation, such as parts of the USA or the Middle East, the control of both air and radiant solar gains are considered to be the most important thermal design criteria. On the other hand, in cool climates, such as Scandinavia, the control of heat loss in a building is considered a more important design parameter. However, it is obvious that by adopting either one of these solutions, the building will be left with an energy handicap in the opposite season. This is especially important in climates such as Central Europe where the control of solar heat gain in the summer may be as important as good thermal insulation in the winter. As a result, excess building services are installed to make up for the inadequacies of the building fabric. This is an unnecessary and inefficient response.

If we took our lead from nature, we would realise that the best way to optimise the climatic benefits is to have a building envelope that positively interacts with its environment. An intelligent and adaptable building skin would regulate the energy flow through itself. It would no longer be a barrier between 'inside' and 'outside', but would become an interface between two energy sinks. Such a skin should be able to tune itself to provide the ideal thermal response to any given set of external climatic conditions, occupancy requirements, orientation and building type.

Theory into Practice
Building engineering is dominated by natural phenomena: gravity and wind forces, temperature and humidity, light and sound, air quality and movement, vibration and reverberation. The building structure and the envelope are used to channel and divert adverse loads to create an internal environment geared to building function, providing lighting, heating, cooling, sound modulation and fresh air for the comfort of the occupants.

Structural and environmental engineers use their knowledge of the behaviour of materials to create a building of load-carrying and climate-moderating characteristics. Our principal goal is an engineering one; to engineer the architect's vision in its design form using all the skills and resources of the engineering profession and using materials and technologies in an environmentally sensitive way.

Our future lies in bridging the gap between 'art and science', 'belief and proof' and 'emotion and measurement'. Contemporary architecture cannot progress without both.

Architecture is a living progressive art generated through the close collaboration of the architect and the engineer. Its success is a measurement of the

An OPAL (omni-purpose apparatus for LEP – large electron-positron collider) detector at CERN (Conseil Européen pour la Recherche Nucléaire) the European centre for particle physics near Geneva

architect/artist's vision and the engineer/scientist's ability to justify that vision.

The architectural profession (architects, artists, engineers and scientists) must maintain a neutral art and science platform for the exchange of views and ideas with special emphasis on encouraging and enhancing interdisciplinary technology transfer, to secure a vision for the future.

Footfalls echo in the memory
down the passage which we did not take
towards the door we have never opened
TS Eliot, Four Quartets

Building engineering should be a complete design service incorporating structural, mechanical, electrical, public health, acoustic, energy, wind, light and environmental facade engineering for buildings. The key to the success of this approach is the involvement of engineers at the earliest stages of design; where air, light, materials and systems may be discussed in depth prior to any design decisions. During our last five years together we have dissolved our differences as structural and services engineers and formed a new design approach with international architects; a design approach initiated by Will Alsop and nurtured at Arups. Our approach is less about solving the problem of say, integrating the passage of air ducts through the structural zone, and more about the 'mystery' of using the thermal inertia of the structure as a climate moderator. This is an attempt to eliminate the need for air conditioning altogether.

Technical Progress enhanced by Technology Transfer

Man has witnessed six technical revolutions. The first was precipitated by basic tasks such as cutting down a tree with a stone. Such activity prompted the manufacture of simple tools. The next revolution can be identified by the initiative which involved the extraction of metals from stone. Different types of stone yielded different metals, each possessing specific properties making them suitable for some functions and not for others. The energy revolution manifested itself in the discovery of machines which could be driven without dependence on natural forces. Mass production made all previous technologies affordable to all. Electronic advances made communication possible without displacement and finally, molecular science enabled man to build form from molecular transformation.

Architecture is traditional. It may have reached an energy revolution, but it is not very efficient. It has little to do with mass production, electronics and/or molecular revolutions. High-tech architecture is fool's gold. How can we compare our elementary successes to those of genetic engineering? With some relief we may accept that even the most *modern* buildings of this century are no more than traditional in the face of technological development.

The ways in which structure and environment interact with each other can be very complex. This is rarely the case in building engineering. The most complex building envelope is technically relatively simple compared with, for example, an aircraft shell. In addition to its structural design which must withstand extremes of pressure and heat; the aircraft shell must be as light and streamlined as possible. A combination of these qualities allows it to carry the largest possible number of passengers in safety and comfort with the least possible amount of engine thrust.

The most highly industrialised objects – on wheels, in flight or fixed on the ground – are most subject to renewal and constantly improve in quality, even in terms of price
Jean Prouvé

The lesson of the aeroplane is not primarily in the form it has created
Le Corbusier, 1946

In the 66 years between the Wright brothers' first flight and the lunar module landing, the technology of our building industry – compared to aeronautics – has progressed comparatively little. In the fields of aerospace, surface transportation, electronics and medicine, technical progress has been widespread and continuous. These technologies are concerned with attaining the maximum possible performance with the minimum materials. Their success rests on the constant search for improved product performance which requires substantial research and development. Instead of following the lead of others and being invigorated by the challenge of change, the industry has built itself into a cul-de-sac. So what is the way forward? How may we engineer technical progress for human benefit?

The future does not necessarily lie in applying selective technologies to an existing fabric concept, that is: window, wall, floor, roof etc. It will come by re-examining the role of the facade and then applying available technologies from other industries worldwide in the most relevant manner. Stone castles in their day shone out as technical beacons in their surroundings. (Intelligent buildings of their time.) Their technical achievement was naturally adopted in the construction of churches and then by commerce and housing. The construction challenge of castles presented military engineers with a clear goal. That goal was survival. Today technical achievements in military projects such as the space shuttle, have influenced other industries but as yet these discoveries have not effected dramatic changes in the field of architecture.

The new goal is world environmental survival. Buildings contribute to over half of the total CO_2 emissions into the atmosphere. It is therefore crucial that the unique skills associated with military technology play a major role in developing the architecture of tomorrow. With the demise for the need for military hardware there is certainly no shortage of design expertise waiting to be employed within the building industry.

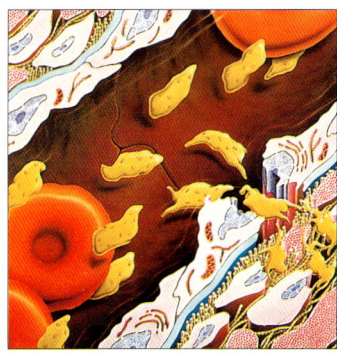

ABOVE: Self repair of damaged blood vessels; BELOW: Protective enclosure; OPPOSITE: Joseph Wright of Derby, The Alchemist in Search of the Philosopher's Stone, *1771/75, oil on canvas*

Engineering Technology Transfer for Future Climatic Control in Architecture: Multi-Source Synthesis

For most modern buildings, technology exists in the shadow of other disciplines and thus the designs are often lacking in terms of a comprehensive, well integrated theory. Often they are not exactly a holistic body of ideas, but opaque and fragmented, without technical substance. This limbo period of design may be overcome through exploration of new directions. This would shape the future of architecture by revitalising a transfer of building technology from other industries. The great virtue of multi-source synthesis in terms of physical material and intellectual resources, is that it is by definition the 'synergetic' multi-source synthesis which is a primary component of technology advancement and the platform for tomorrow's vision.

We are presently associated with a number of research and development initiatives, the objective being to transfer the technical benefits from the manufacturing industry to the building industry. The projects have particular reference to materials and systems which are able to adjust their structural, geometrical, thermal, transparent and porous capabilities when exposed to climatic changes. Such dynamic environmental systems may eventually be able to provide adequate interaction with the climate; eliminating dependence on secondary services which create a satisfactory internal climate. This will result in a new era of building envelope design and in greater internal and external environmental comfort.

In particular, we are reviewing the building engineering possibilities of five types of dynamic environmental responsive systems: geometrical response, thermal response, transparent response, porous response and self maintenance.

Geometrical Response: There are a number of examples which may be adapted for use in the building industry. A shape memory structural material is being researched in the aerospace industry for repairing inaccessible structural damage. It may be moulded into a specific shape and after being injected into position, it will return to its designed shape. These shape memory materials may be used as structural couplers to eliminate axial shortening or extension of elements. Active suspension systems have been developed by army tank manufacturers so that the gun-barrel of the tank remains level as the tank travels at high speed across rough terrain. NASA is experimenting with a similar contraption for the reflectors of one of the largest radio telescopes in the world. The supports re-adjust 60 times a second. Responsive gas piston systems are being developed for earthquake supports, so that as the piston is compressed, the resultant expansion of gas in system reacts against the applied load. Electronic couplers thermally expand when experiencing a com-pressive stress and thermally contract when experiencing tensile stress. For centuries, naval architects have been developing anti-rolling devices to ensure guns and missiles remain level. These systems are now incorporated into off-shore structures to eliminate movement.

Thermal Response: Thermochrome materials are being developed which have a reversible transmittance change dependent on temperature. Thermal-photo-electrical coatings have been invented which become cooler as the sun becomes stronger.

Optical Response: Photochromic materials have been developed which alter their chemical properties with light intensity. In one example 'photogram' glass is doped with the crystal silver halide. Upon the application of light it shows a reversible change in transmission from 86 per cent to 22 per cent during hours of continuous sunshine. Electrochromic materials are being developed in the USA, Japan and Europe. The material has reversible colour change capabilities activated by applying a low voltage. These materials have a unique market value as a low maintenance, controllable shading device.

Porosity Response: A number of clothing materials have been developed which allow free movement of air across the fabric while inhibiting the flow of moisture, thus creating a rainproof envelope with ventilation; eg, Gortex and Syntex.

Self Maintenance: The nuclear fuel industry world wide has been developing a number of sophisticated maintenance robots. These robots are now being adapted to aid the construction, maintenance and repair of buildings. In Japan, they have developed a robot which is able to climb the tiled facade of a building, find damaged tiles and replace them.

If we study these innovations and implement them as a matter of course, we will begin to develop a pattern of building and a desire to work within an interdisciplinary team. This would lead to a truly 'highly technical' architecture.

Engineering Architectural Vision

One of the architectural visions which we are beginning to develop in more detail is that of the Monolithic Building Envelope, which is a product of this integrated approach to the design. Like the medieval castle, it has its form, structure, skin, services and finish integrated as one.

The technology already exists to develop an intelligent monolithic building envelope. The enclosure could, in effect, be a multi-functional 'skin' that would build and maintain itself, and respond to climatic changes such as wind, sun, rain and temperature, whilst creating a building which would be self-sufficient in energy demands. The building skin would have to perform specific functions. It would respond to applied loads and regulate the energy flow. This is achieved by collecting available free energy, distributing it where required and storing or dissipating the rest. This provides a com-

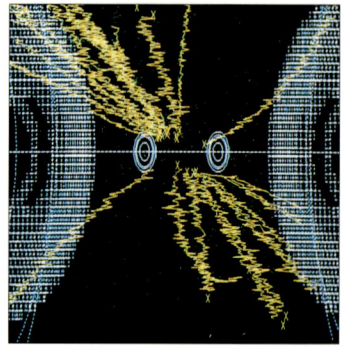

ABOVE: Model of Singapore Tower, Alsop and Stormer; BELOW: Computer simulation of particle collision in the OPAL detector at CERN

munication interface between inside and outside.

The monolithic enclosure of the future may be a fabric with various weaves of thread such as: structural veins responding to applied loads and sensors. These would be connected to the 'brain' which monitors both the internal and external environment. Energy collectors are essential for the storage of extra energy and through variable radiation control, the weave will also control the colour of the enclosure. Thermal response control is activated by the solar spectrum and the thermal emission of the skin, as well as making use of the 'atmospheric window'. Thermoelectric weaves could use the energy collected to provide cooling or heating on demand. In addition to these inventions there are acoustic absorbers, reflectors, anti-noise devices, ventilation, porosity patches and construction and reconstruction arteries.

The whole building system would be controlled by a main computer or brain. This brain would continually monitor signals from the sensors and adjust the geometry, thermal and light response accordingly. This would be combined with the output of the thermoelectric panel, to maintain the required set points. This is the thermogeneous and fully integrated design that incorporates plant and fabric as one – an 'environmental mediator'. A new wardrobe of aesthetic expressions would be made available. A monolithic enclosure skin would give the architect and the engineer the same magical powers as the chameleon, changing to suit the environment. They would become the artists who, with their palate of digitised colours and the building facade as a canvas, could follow the moods of architectural fashion and maintain an engineering ideal at will.

Self Assessment

Modern architecture has reached a watershed in the post-industrial revolution as it begins to experience the full impact of the scientific revolution. The architectural profession needs to debate their future role in an ever changing society. It spends too much effort eliminating internal competition in an attempt to defend individual, popular artistic methods. In the meantime, people have lost faith in building technology and have sought comfort and reassurance in applications of art over technology, giving an illusion of technical performance that is artful but tech-less. The up shot has been the devaluation of the engineers' contribution to the design of buildings. There is no doubt that the building industry has had its technical failures, but in reaction some have abandoned engineering excellence at the expense of practical expediency.

The profession is in danger of de-skilling itself; engineers without direction or a guiding vision from clients and architects, are finding that their skills and interests are beginning to waste away. The art of performance building relies on the thorough and complete co-operation of the whole design team under the leadership of the architect.

To secure a vision of modern architecture, we will have to understand the art of technical performance in terms of maximising material, energy and skills for the benefit of mankind – only then will we have something to celebrate!

Formerly with Ove Arup & Partners, Battle McCarthy engineer the interaction of materials and system with climatic forces in architecture and urban design

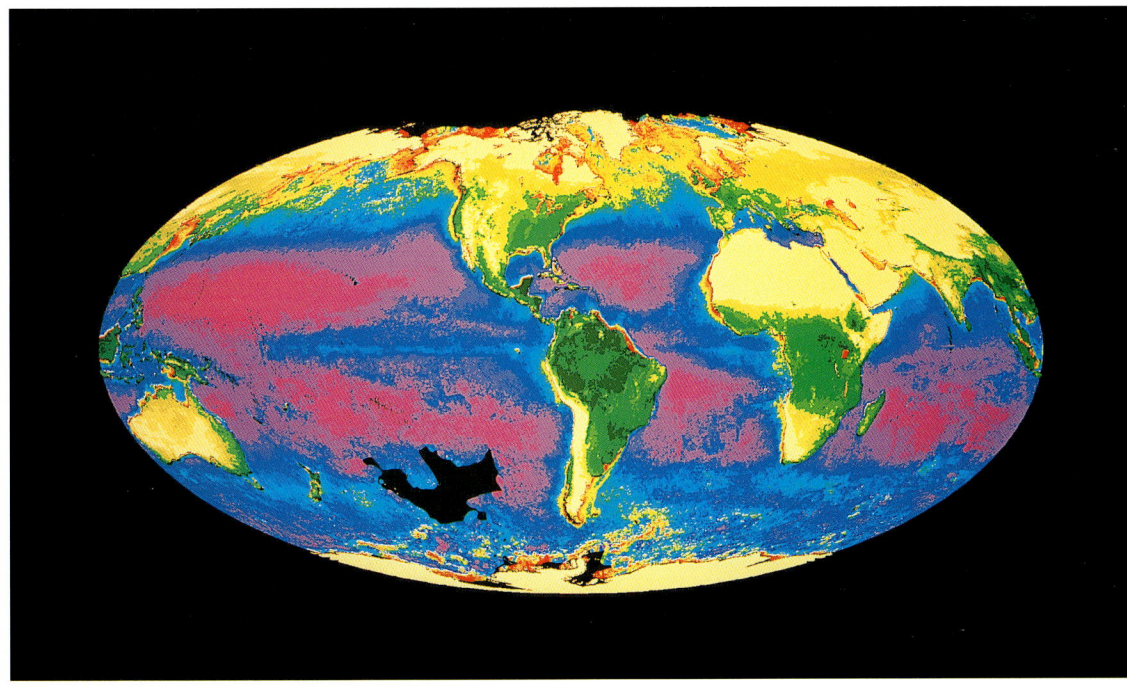

False colour composite satellite image of Earth's biosphere, showing the distribution of vegetation on land and of phytoplankton in the oceans

HANS HELMS
THE CITY SHAKEN

From its inception, the market economy, alias the capitalist system, has been plagued by internally generated contradictions. These inherent contradictions became most obvious when the social order called communism or socialism, which had been conceived as an alternative to capitalism, abolished itself, having become eroded and corrupted by the folly and ambition of its *nomenklatura*. No matter how weak, indecisive and defective the experiment had turned out to be, even in its deformed shape it acted internally as well as externally as a corrective upon capitalist societies.

After the collapse of the socialist alternative, any attempt at ideologically camouflaging capitalism has become superfluous. The contradictions shaking the capitalist system manifest themselves now in a noticeably cruder manner. Qualified minorities in every single society from the First to the Third World are no longer willing to close their eyes. Gradually they begin to suspect the contradictions which the system continually produces. Those watchful minorities begin to surmise that sooner or later the contradictions, if not checked in time will, by necessity, lead to disastrous consequences. However, both the complexity and the brutality of the contradictory process let critical observers shy away from a concise analysis of the causes and prevent them from arriving at the unavoidable conclusion that this system is unreformable and must be fought on a political level. Erroneous feelings of impotence have caused a lethargy so that the democratic decision processes are on the brink of total deterioration.

The Lords of Big Capital exult and work at persuading the salaried and wage-earning people that capitalism has won its final and irreversible victory. In their exuberant view there is absolutely no obstacle which would prevent the capitalist powers from exploiting the human race for the sole purpose of profit maximisation – whether reaping in exorbitant profits makes any sense or not. They believe that there are no critical groups and individuals left who would have the desire and the power of conviction to oppose the system seriously. The remaining one-twelfth of the human race which Big Capital needs for relaxing the surplus value, will be rewarded and humoured by being thrown into a lifelong stressful but lucrative competition for vain and unnecessary consumer riches.

Nowhere does the capitalist system break up with such grave consequences as in the urban centres and urbanised wastelands. It is here that the system regenerates itself in the most contradictory and repercussive ways. Many centralised and federal states are indebted up to several times their respective gross national product. A multitude of communities are weighed down by debts, so that their tax income is hardly sufficient for paying off the accruing interest rates. Burdened metropolises such as Berlin, New York City, Manila and Mexico City are becoming entangled ever more insolubly in perennial financial straits. Even comparatively well-off cities such as Milan or Munich, Birmingham or Barcelona, Duisburg or Antwerp, would have to file for bankruptcy if they did not resort to dubious financial manipulations and to issuing a growing flood of bonds on the global capital markets. The tax income of communities in the newly colonised areas of Eastern Germany and the countries of Eastern Europe, is so low that it barely covers the bottom of their coffers. In the worst cases they fall victim to national chauvinist excesses where the allure of big money is rekindling.

In the era of the credit card, most communities are operating and building on credit in remarkably thoughtless ways. Fiercely competing with each other for the benevolent patronage of small and big investors, they have erected, usually under 'social' pretexts, image-laden major public buildings without any sound cost-benefit-analysis whatsoever.

To their eternal glory, city fathers and mothers have built themselves some respectable city-hall-fortresses, imposing museums, splendid theatres or high-tech multi-purpose halls. They have driven subways and high capacity motorways straight through the core of their municipalities. They have gained popularity by building swimming halls and pools, football stadia and sports arenas. At best, a tiny fraction of the expenditures for these public buildings came from the budget; the larger part of the millions and billions spent had to be raised on the capital markets by floating high-yield, cost intensive communal bonds. Dividends rise and fall with the fluctuations of the economy and in a recession they might be cancelled altogether. Interest rates for gilt-edged communal paper, however, always remains on the same high level. Meanwhile, quite a few of those prestigious communal projects have reached the stage of gradual progressive decay. The interest payments are still continuing, the construction costs have not yet been paid in full, but now there are hardly any budgetary

View of Canary Warf, London

funds available to finance the most urgent repairs without getting even deeper into debts. Consequently, the decay advances.

Even in boom times, such continuous financial burdens cannot be tolerated. In a phase of deep recession like the present one they push communities into ruin. Each economic cycle aggravates the situation. The immediate and visible effect: swimming halls, libraries and hospitals are being closed down by the dozen; bridges, streets, sewer systems and other public utilities will be patched up, if at all, in a rather desultory manner: the decay progresses.

In this desolate situation, privatisation appears to be a magic way out: it seems to make the state regional and municipal problems vanish into thin air. However, the disposal of municipal buildings and public utilities, usually puts only a fraction of the original cost back into the city coffers. The slender proceeds rarely suffice to liquidate the financial commitments of yesteryear. Quite definitely, squandering of municipal real estate makes its future uses more expensive. The purchasers want to reap profits from their properties. If these fail to materialise there will definitely be provisions in the sales agreement allowing certain types of misuse or demolition and subsequent new construction. In somewhat more civilised countries such as Denmark, the Netherlands, France and Switzerland, such squandering of municipal real estate may yet be the exception. In highly deregulated market economies such as the US, Canada, Great Britain and now also in Germany's recently acquired Eastern federal states, squandering of public property has become common practice.

Privatisation of public property for the purpose of filling out budget holes is mostly preceded by extensive personnel cutbacks: from the police via the fire service, street cleaning, garbage collection, the library and hospital staff down to the most obscure city departments, the public services are being decimated because the communities lack the funds for wages and salaries. This happened in New York City right after the so-called financial crisis in the mid 70s during the early years of the Koch administration, and now it is happening again in a much more radical fashion under Mayor Dinkins. Staff cuts in the public services have an aggravating and barbarising effect upon life and work in the city. Staff reductions increase the army of the unemployed and unemployment puts a grave strain on the city budget.

Never before, not even during the Great Depression, did New York City have as many unemployed as today: 28.5 per cent; 2 million out of the 7.2 million citizens. Never before, not even in the era from 1890 to 1930 when immigrants from Eastern and Southern Europe pushed into the city in large numbers, did as many New Yorkers live beneath the poverty line – well over 25 per cent or more than 1.8 million people.

According to *Business Week* (18 May 1992) modern pauperism tends to concentrate in the 'centre cities': 42 per cent – almost half of all the poor in the US – live in the large cities in the national and regional metropolitan areas and many of them are homeless. This implies that resulting from the recession and from mass unemployment, big city budgets have become disproportionally and excessively burdened. In the first place, the cities lose a large percentage of their gross municipal product: it simply remains non-produced. *Business Week* estimates this loss to exceed $60 billion for all US cities. In the second place, the cities miss out on the taxes which they would receive if this part of the gross municipal product were to be produced. Thirdly, the cities have to raise additional $120 billion for welfare payments. At present, New York City has to support 1.2 million welfare recipients that are 18 per cent of its population. In many other communities in the US and in most European countries the situation is similar if not worse. The global war between rich and poor over the distribution of the gross global product is raging now with brute force on both sides in the urban centres of the First World. What else would be the reason for the recent aimless and utterly self-destructive uprising of the blacks in the ghettos of Los Angeles and of many other US metropolitan areas, or the multiracial revolt among the unemployed youth in Bristol, Huddersfield and elsewhere in the UK. This civil war of the poor against the well-to-do is not only a result of increasing mass and long-term unemployment and of a life without any perspective, but is a consequence of the cities' financial problems and also of private capital's disinvestment in the cities. Together they produce decay of the infrastructure and of real estate in the big cites. The tax paying middle classes and their employers flee from the decay in the centre to suburbia. The poor and underprivileged stay behind in the core cities. Simultaneously, strategically well situated central areas in the big cities undergo gentrification: yuppies on relatively high income levels displace their poor sisters and brothers and force them into the slums which are already overcrowded. Exodus from the cities and gentrification are interrelated, though counteractive processes which split the cities even more radically into 'dual cities' for the rich and the poor. Today, a small number of sparkling islands of prosperity are floating in the midst of a sea of utter poverty and progressive decay.

Regardless of the social system in which it takes place, technological progress permanently obsolesces the spheres of production, distribution, communications, administration, services, and consumption, as well as their respective workplaces. That is to say, technological progress obsolesces a more or less extensive number of the respective installations in each city. To a lesser degree it affects the existing buildings which can be adapted to new uses with relatively modest amounts of money and cleverness. To a larger degree it affects the destruction of workplaces within the urban space and the logistics of the users.

In capitalism, town planners rarely knew how to make timely and pertinent organisational provisions for the changes of use to the urban space as these resulted from technological progress. Neither have capitalist societies ever been very successful in properly channelling technological progress in socially and urbanistically tolerable or even beneficial ways. Capital and real estate interests which tend to act as a rather compact collective in spite of a diversity of conflicts and contradictions, block intelligent urban planning. Big Capital's uncompromising urge to maximise profit at almost any cost, blocks society's channelling efforts. As a result, urban planning has reacted to technological progress hesitantly. Restricted by the concentrated power of the combined capital and real estate interests, it has not been strong and independent enough to develop offensive planning strategies and carry them through. Well-planned decentralisation within the social and urban functional sectors would have been well worth striving for because it would have prevented the boundless increase of the number of cars and trucks circulating on congested roads. Instead of doing that, society permitted random urban sprawl to gain ground and little is more destructive for nature, human beings and cities big and small.

By virtue of integrating the computer and communication systems into global networks, it became technically feasible around 1980 to control decentralisation trends for the benefit of urban coherence. Unfortunately, nothing of this kind was done; for example, in the 1950s, capitalist societies subjected themselves to the automobile system and stupidly destroyed the structure and coherence of their cities by brutally adapting them to the needs of the automobile. Rapidly proliferating high technologies have a number of repercussions on urban development: one is progressive urban sprawl which results in decentralised, totally amorphous agglomerations, such as London, Brussels, Zurich or Frankfurt; another is the unchecked elephantine growth of mega-municipalities such as Houston or Los Angeles. These defective urban developments disavow any attempt at precautionary planning; neither do they permit later meaningful corrections.

Analysed in terms of political economy, it seems rather unlikely that cities and urbanised regions shaken by technological and economic cycles will have a chance to survive unless they resort to fundamental structural modifications and major functional restrictions. Urban structures are in a process of dissolution. This process set in when societies and their cities succumbed to the automobile. Those urban fragments which miraculously have stayed more or less intact are on the verge of sinking into the morass of chaotic agglomeration. Lethargic as we are, we will just go on using our communities and urbanised regions in the reckless manner established long ago which has become so very familiar and comfortable. We will go on overlooking the discrepancies and contradictions in our behaviour until all of a sudden we will realise that our urban environment is collapsing all around us. If we want to prevent this we will have to understand the following: we should not tolerate the control which the military establishment in complicity with financial capital exert over the sciences, technology, the economy and urban development, as if it were their private sphere of interest. The storm clouds of financial speculation which at this moment are hovering over the peaks of downtown office skyscrapers, may soon discharge themselves as hurricanes and together with the hot-air balloons inflated by stock deals, they may sweep away the entire capitalist system to which we owe the present state of affairs. Eventually the earth might defend itself from the mortal blows which we are dealing out with mounting force. Since the inception of the industrial revolution we have considered this our right.

Excerpt from the paper given by Hans Helm at the sixth International Bauhaus-Colloquium in Weimar, Germany, 18-20 June 1992.

View of Tokyo

MAXWELL HUTCHINSON
RETHINKING THE FUTURE

Your ruler Jupiter is now in a contrary mood, so keep a tight rein on your spending, and on your tongue, or you could offend somebody who means well. Romance preoccupies you from the 15th when Mars and Venus are in tune, but look before you leap: a revelation from a friend on the 13th could show the object of your affections in a new and unexpected light.
Sagittarius (23 November- 22 December) Wanda Starr, UK Vogue, March 1993.

Astrologers have the unenviable task of gilding the future with enticing excitement, reassuring uncertainty and eternal optimism. The credentials of their inexact, dubious and empirical science does not seem to diminish in the panoply of popular culture. No tabloid or glossy would be complete without its Star Gazer. Expensive phone-in telephone services update astrological uncertainty with predictable rapidity. Mutual contradiction between and amongst the community of divining mystics only appears to increase our enthusiasm for their vacuous rambling.

I defy anyone with the vaguest interest in matters of the spirit and the soul to bypass an astrological prediction without so much as a glance. Indeed if *The Times* of London sought to become even more popularist I guess even 'The Thunderer' would entice more than half a handful of readers to dwell idly (and with more than a little embarrassment) on its aristocratic astrologer. It would seem that all of us have a quaint but human preoccupation with the future. Any why not? That which has been writ, is written. All news is old news. The past holds no excitement: it is anticipation in reverse. As the clock ticks with quartz synchronicity around the globe, we all want to be one step ahead. One second might just make the difference: a road accident; a cardiac arrest; a terrorist bomb in a dustbin; an envelope with the lottery win of a lifetime.

If one minute's clairvoyance can do all that, how much more a decade or two's confident prognostication could do. A politician who could confidently predict the pattern of society, the value of his country's currency, the balance of world power and his own popularity, would surely escalate his authority to world domination. A scientist who could accelerate his experiments (in a quantum leap) to bypass the time-consuming but essential labours of research, could control the world with the same certainty as his crystal gazing political master.

The military strategist who could join battle with the certain knowledge of success could lay waste a foe without a twinge of conscience; for victory was preordained and the means, by definition, justified the predictable end.

So, naturally, and as part of the human condition, we all desire to gaze into the kaleidoscope of the future in a vain attempt to reconcile the inevitability of the present with the tantalising mystery of the future. No more so than in architecture and the environment. In point of fact the majority of professional futurologists (a contradiction in terms if ever I heard one) have dwelt on where, how and in what manner we live, more than on any other quotient of the human condition. Scientists, philosophers, and to a lesser extent theologians, deal with the human condition here and now. Those who raise their eyes above the horizon inevitably glimpse a building or two amongst their predicted matrix of change.

Since the median of the Victorian era the optimistic view of change has radically changed in itself. A stodgy and complacent optimism framed the British attitude of the 1850s. Great Britain, thanks to the enterprise of manufacturers and merchants, was wealthier than ever. The workshop of the world was the paradise of a successful bourgeoisie governed by a bourgeois Queen and an efficient Prince Consort. Joseph Paxton's Crystal Palace for the Great Exhibition of 1851 was the outstanding example of mid-19th century iron and glass architecture. It thronged with thousands of visitors who marvelled at the size of the building and quantity of products on show. As the official catalogue of the exhibition asserted: 'An event like this exhibition could not have taken place at any other period, and perhaps not among any other people than ourselves.' The diminutive but genuinely visionary Prince Albert set the future agenda of the exhibition in his preparatory address: 'Nobody who has paid any attention to the particular features of the present era will doubt for a moment that we are living in a period of most wonderful transition, which tends rapidly to the accomplishment of that great end to which indeed all history points, the realisation for the unity of mankind.' Robust Victorian optimism seasoned with arrogant certainty.

Save for the mould-breaking structural and architectural majesty of Paxton's pavilion, the Exhibition of 1851 would go all but forgotten in the history of architecture, design and the design sciences. As Nikolaus Pevsner put it: 'The aesthetic

Scene from the film Blade Runner, *directed by Ridley Scott, 1982*

quality of the products was abominable. Sensible visitors realised that, and soon discussion started in England and other countries as to the reasons for such an evident failure. It is easy for us, today [1936] to enumerate various such reasons; but it was hard indeed for a generation that had grown up amid unprecedented discovery in science and technique. There were the new railways and power-looms, there were the cunning inventions to facilitate the production of almost any object formally made so laboriously by craftsman – why should these wonderful improvements not help to improve art as well?'[1] The great engineers, Paxton, Telford and Brunell had set the agenda and established the optimistic parameters for the future. The designers and architects still languished in the past. In 'The Battle of the Styles', the dubious aesthetic counter-values of classicism and the gothic were fought over like the non-existent boundaries of middle Europe, for prizes not worth the effort or the manpower. And the visionary engineers knew it. Whilst the aesthetes bickered and quarrelled amongst themselves the technocrats planned a visionary future with little or no place for the humanities, the arts and certainly not architecture.

A hundred years later in 1951, when post-war Britain sought a two-fold celebration of victory in the Second World War and it was the 100th anniversary of the Great Exhibition, the helmsmen on this occasion were drawn from the ranks of architects – probably more out of fashion and convenience, as their engineering and technological colleagues could not be bothered with something as superficial and flippant as a six month exhibition on the south bank of the Thames. There were roads to build, disease to conquer, rocketry and computerisation to master and, coincidentally, the world had yet to get to grips with the geo-universal impact of Einstein's new mathematics, the second law of relativity and quantum mechanics.

Once again, the scientists and technocrats were carefully and surreptitiously planning and gazing into the future whilst the men with the suede shoes and bow ties whiled away the peace-time muse they thought they deserved.

If dancing the afternoon away outside the Dome of Discovery in the shadow of Powell and Moya's skylon, to the strains of Joe Loss and the Boys was second heaven, then first heaven on the agenda was right there in the *Homes and Gardens* pavilion with its backdrop mural by John Piper. Everything had spindly legs. And balls on. The more 'outre' and 'moderne' the better. A strange English interpretation of German modernism mutated through five years in khaki. The more Formica, Bakelite, linoleum, vermiculite, nylon and neon, the better. Meanwhile, over the river at Imperial College, the true intellectuals of Mother Science set our controls for the heart of the sun, without a thought about the cut of their trousers or the haute couture of their coffee table.

A hundred years had changed the entire world beyond recognition. The all pervasive view of the future was still optimistic. The agenda was set by science and technology and conveniently arranged and dressed up by the nancy boys at the drawings boards in the studios. The language to which the designers gravitated was that of science fiction and space travel. William Feaver put it like this: 'For the ordinary . . . visitor . . . crossing the Thames by Bailey Bridge, spurred on by Richard Huw's flickering ornamental spinners, was like time-travelling. On the far side lay the gleaming perspectives of tomorrow. The South Bank had an air of touchdown, the Dome (of Discovery) a flying saucer, the skylon on its zigzag supports ready to be catapulted to the stars, the main concourse embedded with a criss-cross pattern of landing lights, the line up of fountains at the near end splashing a welcome . . . Here, beyond doubt, was the Township of the Future, the sort of place Dan Dare strove to defend in 1999 from the appalling Treens of the Red Moon, masterminded by the tiny green-headed Mekon.'[2] So, in 1951, as in 1851, the tone was optimism, the key note was technology, the driving traction, science and the dominant philosophy existential agnostic humanism.

In 1993 we are increasingly obsessed with the millennium; an inconsequential date if ever there was one. If there is anything certain about the millennium it is *not* the two thousandth anniversary of the birth of Jesus Christ. Even if it were, this is hardly a reason to set aside Hogmanay in 2000 for a certain celebration. For the followers of Jesus Christ, every Christmas and every Easter is a millenic event in itself. Popularism demands that world civilisation anchors its time frame into the culture of established Christendom regardless of religion or philosophy.

Let's take 2051 – two hundred years on from the Great Exhibition and one hundred years after the Festival of Britain – as a point of departure. If we ever get there, His Royal Highness the Prince of Wales and I would be a mere 103 years old. A Prime Minister in 2051, who would have reached the age of 55 has yet to be born in the year 1996. If medical science accelerates its unnecessary quest for the promotion of human longevity I may just be there.

Architects have a vocational responsibility to speculate about the future; in fact, to do more than speculate, to have genuine concern, carry out research, integrate existing information, proselytise, set out harsh polemic, draw cartoons and challenge the natural conservatism of the status quo. This is part of their metier.

In a pair of decades dominated by reactionary conservatism it is important to call to mind TS Eliot's words of 1934: 'We are always in danger, in clinging to an old tradition, or attempting to re-establish one, of confusing the vital and the unessential, the real and sentimental. What we can do is use our minds, remembering that a tradition without intelligence is not worth having, to discover what is the best life for us, not as a political abstraction, but as a particular people in a particular place.'

Gerald K O'Neill is an optimistic futurist. He has identified two essential aspects of star gazing particularly relevant to the architectural predicament.[3] Firstly, any worthwhile prognostication can only be based on available information. '. . . Most aspects of the human situation can't be very different from what they are now, for change (except for sudden catastrophes) takes time. And well beyond the horizon of a century any predictions we can make are sure to fall short of reality, because by then discoveries that we do not now even suspect will begin to affect the development of civilisation profoundly.' O'Neill goes on to assert a second and profound thesis. 'To find out what "will be in any case" and what "could be if we try" I began by studying what was said by the crystal gazers of the past . . . In every type of futuristic writing, from the impersonal to the subjective, I found the same pattern: most prophets overestimated how much the world would be transformed by social and political change and underestimated the forces of technological change.'

So O'Neill leavens our enthusiasm for prediction by reminding us that we can only predict the future outcome of events based on our current knowledge and that those who have had the audacity and courage to predict in the past have underdone science and overdone social benefit and change. Tempted as I am to dive into the world of divine omniscience and foreknowledge, the architectural mandate for prediction is a human one. At its worst reactionary, sentimental and historicist, at its best consummately informed by the state of science and technology and, God willing, divinely inspired.

En route to a vision of 2051, we stop off at a couple of Star Dates on the way. 1965 was International Co-operation Year. The architectural battle in that year of co-operation and fraternity was grasped with alacrity by Richard Buckminster Fuller who set out his agenda for the World Design Science Decade 1965-1975 on the pages of this magazine in August 1965. In his typically verbose, obtuse, but poetically incisive manner, Fuller gazed down the telescope with the same optimism which exemplified the Prince Consort's exhortations on the Great Exhibition. 'In the next decade's worldising of industrial production systems and energy generating and transmission systems, we will witness the surprise solution to the establishment of world citizenship occasioned swiftly and simply by multiplication of world passenger traffic to magnitudes which will necessitate credit-card type passports and automation of omni-border clearances; plus the amplification of the efficiencies accruing to common market.' Clearly, Fuller in Gerald O'Neill's terms once again over estimated the capacity of society to ride the scientific tidal wave of change. If he knew the petty bickerings of today's common market he would be appalled at the abuse of his principle credo of 65: 'The world's prime vital problem bears repeating a million times. It is: how to triple swiftly, safely, and satisfyingly, the overall performance realisation per pound, kilowatts, and man hours of the world's comprehensive resource . . . Doing vastly more with vastly and invisibly less is know technically as ephemeralisation. The mass production of electronic controls inaugurated automation. With automation has come a dawning awareness of the invisible avalanche of ephemeralisation.'

Fuller took science and technology as his point of departure. Seven years later, after a decade or more of published polemic, Peter Cook and Archigram approached the future through suitably round, rose coloured glasses.[4] 'Our collective mental blockage occurs between the land of the small-scale consumer products and the objects which make up our environment. Perhaps it will not be until such things as housing, amenity place and work place become recognised as consumer products that can be "bought off the peg" – with all this, implies in terms of expandability (foremost), industrialisation, up-to-date-ness, consumer choice, and basic product-design – that we can begin to make an environment that is really part of a developing human culture.'

Our preoccupation today is the setting of architecture in the context of the second centenary of the Great Exhibition. With all this in mind – with scepticism and cynicism, rationality and romanticism insolubly unbalanced – how does the outside world scatter the particles on the architectural map of the future?

Michael Davies, one of Richard Rogers' partners, described the experience of living in a responsive building in the future: 'Look up at a spectrum-washed envelope, whose surface is a map of instantaneous performance, stealing energy from the air with an iridescent shrug, rippling its photo-grids as a cloud runs across the sun, a wall which, as the night chill falls, fluffs up its feathers and, turning white on its north face and blue on the south, closes its eyes but not without remembering to pump a little glow down to the night porter, clear a view-patch for lovers on the south side of level 22 and so turn 12 per cent silver just before dawn.'

The Japanese in their approach to the intelligent house, through study of the linguistically boggling 'Humanwave Engineering', have devised the concept of the 'Home Bus'. They put it, inimitably, like this: 'The Home Bus system (HBS) is a completely new comprehensive and compatible system developed to improve the quality of home life, in the information orientated society of the future. HBS aims at realising a comfortable and creative life by using an in-house network connecting house-hold appliances, including the home computer, and by using a public network connecting the house with a highly advanced social system. Information transmission lines, installed in the home for this purpose, are called the "Home Bus" and we call this the house of the future, "The Intelligent House".'

The UK's British Telecom prognosticate a not dissimilar future for our homes relying on Dr Richard Holti of the Taverstock Institute of Human Relations, who extols the virtues of home teleworking: 'There are no barriers to wholesale teleworking other than psychological barriers.' BT's Director of Public Communication Products, Andy Green, with the consummate arrogance of the technocrat, explains their first experiment in the teleworking: 'The past decade has seen an explosion of new technology. BT's mission is to give everyone that benefit. That's why we are demonstrating in this highly practical way just how advance teleworking now is pointing the way for other companies in Britain and around the world. BT has estimated that by 1995 more than two million Britons could be working from home for at least three days a week. We want to develop the support systems to ease the change in lifestyles. Nowhere in the world has anyone ever used electronic mail and videophones in this way.'

With the Japanese and BT concentrating on the home, IBM International celebrated the tenth anniversary of the personal computer on 18 January 1993: 'History sprinkled with watershed products that arrived in an inchoate market and crystallised a whole new order in which business organisations instinctively altered the way they do things and society is smitten with a new sense of possibilities. These pivotal products often aren't the first, fastest, best or biggest of their kind. They just make sense. The Model T Ford, the Boeing 707, and Cable IV come to mind. Once they appeared, the planet was a different place. A decade ago
IBM unleashed one of these marvels on a ready world. Its PC . . .'

The Shimizu Corporation, predictably of Japan, is the least of all shrinking violets at the future party. 'In response to the coming challenges of construction in space, Shimizu Corporation established its Space Project Office in April 1987, the first organised effort to advance space engineering by a Japanese construction company. With the company's comprehensive strength in fields ranging from architectural design and construction to urban planning, along with its proven technological expertise, Shimizu is confident of its ability to contribute significantly to the field of space development.' This simply means that the Japanese egghead dreamers are planning an incredible range of futuristic options, some of which may even be realised within my modest expectation of life. Firstly, a space station constructed by robotics. Secondly, and more staggeringly, a 'space hotel' which will be in operation by the year 2020. 'The hotel will be the final destination of tours using an 80-seater space plane capable of horizontal take-off and landing. This plane and a simple training programme of only two or three days, could make space trips a recreational pursuit available to the general public.' It doesn't stop there.

'One of the most promising space projects for the early 21st century is the construction of a lunar base. A lunar base would not only contribute considerably to the advance of science but could also serve as a large-scale facility for the production of oxygen and helium-3.'

The drawings and computer models of the Shimizu lunar based concept seem devoid of any genuine architectural or aesthetic influence. The design system and its architectural expression relies upon newly developed Japanese concrete technology: 'The Shimizu solution to the special problems of hydrating cement in a vacuum involves the use of powdered ice and the radiation energy (such as microwaves) to crystallise the curing process.' So man's first moon architecture is going to come straight off the Japanese engineer's drawing board, out of the cement works via the Ice Age and a microwave oven.

Meanwhile, the world architectural community satisfies itself with incestuous arguments about style and the promulgation of one pious and vacuous philosophy after another. The hundredth edition of this magazine celebrated global architectural 'Theory and Experimentation'. The Symposium wallowed in obscurantism and elitism, wantonly grave-robbed every branch of popular philosophy with myopic misunderstanding and focussed architectural futurology on matters of taste, order, colour, cut and line: about as profound as the mind-numbing Paris seasonal collections.

The Sci-Fiers of today are a depressed and depressing lot. They certainly do not share the vision of 1851, or 1951. They have more in common with George Orwell's *1984*. They turn their backs on hotels in space and update the horrific architecture-based world of Fritz Lang's *Metropolis*. Ridley Scott, the director of the iconoclastic film *Blade Runner* (based on the novel by Philip K Dick *Do Androids Dream of Electric Sheep?*), was recently inspired to release a reworking of his movie incorporating footage previously omitted from the original master-work. The look is even more threatening. The decayed architecture dripping in filth, the atmosphere laden with acid rain, the streets crowded with the abandoned and the prurient. Scott's vision of tomorrow is deeply embedded in the failure of architecture, the built environment, to cope with the catastrophic impact of the future so clearly envisaged by Fuller in 1965.

Popular science fiction cinema like the Road Movies and *Alien III* reject the comfortable soap opera, squeaky clean, hierarchy of the 1960s *Star Trek* series now popularly lampooned for its childish mannerism. In the last of the *Alien* films the future is a frightening, lonely, angry, desolate place devoid of any aesthetic satisfaction and with architecture conspicuous by its absence.

If genuine architecture is to respond to the human appetite for prognostication, prediction and vision, it must free itself of its incestuous preoccupation with the simple appearance of the objects it designs and creates. As architectural arguments rage about this that or the other style, silent engineers in Tokyo are planning the real world of 2051. The microwaved concrete of Lunar Base 1 will have as much to do with post-modernism or deconstructivism as its space transport with today's in-vogue Maserati. Architects are the 'theologians' of the environment. They have the ethical duty to set the boundaries of responsibility and define culpability and guilt. This generation has failed to engage with the future in a responsible and meaningful way. As architectural education throws off the burdensome mantle of 1950s academic pomposity, the New Age architects of tomorrow will confidently set their eyes above the temporal travesty of stylistic preference and plan a future of human proportion: on the moon, in my blackguard, and just around the corner. Wherever. For architecture with wings on its heels – the sky's the limit. If we're lucky.

'The RIBA is to debate a motion which would prohibit members from specifying asbestos-related products, as part of a campaign mounted in co-operation with the building worker's union, Ucatt. Councillor Ian Colquhoun said: "We must face the responsibility we have as the conscience of the building industry."' Building Design, 4 March 1983.

Notes
1. Nikolaus Pevsner, Pioneers of Modern Design from William Morris to Walter Gropius, Pelican, 1949.
2. William Feaver, 'Festival Star' from A Tonic to the Nation: The Festival of Britain, Thames and Hudson, 1976, Mary Banham and Bevis Hillier (Eds).
3. Gerald K O'Neill, 2081: A Hopeful View of the Human Future, Jonathan Cape, 1981.
4. Peter Cook, et al (Eds), Archigram, Studio Vista, 1972.

Model of the Shimizu space station project

MICHAEL SPENS
THE NATIONAL WRITING CENTRE AND CITY LIBRARY
Swansea, South Wales

Will Alsop, in winning the competition last February to design the National Writing Centre, has consolidated a reputation that has been built uncompromisingly upon a clear vision of the next century and the architecture that a more open and diversified society will come to demand more and more frequently. The competition itself may prove to have been a watershed in the succession of a new, different generation of architects, even. Alsop is different in age from the high-tech knights by barely half a generation – but the world which he and a supporting cast of architects, engineers, and artists inhabit is several decades apart from the *Eagle* comic inspired adulation of technical parts that launched 'high-tech' as an architectural connotation.

It is significant that the also-rans in this competition final were, among others, Michael Graves and Stirling and Wilford But then the project in hand required an understanding of cultural forces, local aspirations, and no preconceptions as to the nature of a seaside provincial city in South Wales. Alsop already had an inkling, since his Cardiff Bay Visitors' Centre attracted some 200,000 visitors in its first year – the ability to attract such a community to the extent that it identifies with the building on offer and even wants to hang onto it. Alsop buildings do not descend on the community from on high. Instead they establish an affinity, a feeling of collaboration in the question of the future.

The competition brief was a remarkably enlightened one, devoid of the usual bureaucratic priorities. The project was to incorporate a major new central library building, but only in its second phase. The initial phase demanded a more challenging array of facilities, including exhibition galleries to accommodate a Museum of the Word, a range of changing displays, an international writers' centre carrying overnight accommodation (libraries are conducive to sleep and dreams), plus a network of activity space, linked also to a cafe/restaurant and a major bookshop. Here was an extraordinary example, in Britain, of a city council determined to stimulate a wide spectrum of literary culture, yet in a deep relationship not dependent upon adjacent academia. The Word, in Swansea has been most prevalent when it has sprung from the streets and pubs and bedsits, conscious always of Dylan Thomas (and Richard Burton) in this way, the life of Kingsley Amis as lived hereby is no less relevant, endorsing along the way the predictions of Richard Hoggart (written, it must be remembered, at much the same time as the *Eagle* comic was created). Alsop didn't have that deep knowledge of the place, but he had the intelligence (and humility) to involve Mel Gooding, who comes from deep within.

The result has been a remarkable affirmation of hope in the cultures of tomorrow. Woven into the concept is a full consideration of available cultural networks upon which the physical structure required can enrich and regenerate itself. Fundamental has been the awareness of the Swansea City authorities that they have, for a long time, been sitting on seams not just of black gold, but of literary gold. The question was how to extract the resource in a viable way.

At this juncture it is worth recalling that Alsop had, two years past, given due consideration to the Museum of Scotland requirements for an extension. The purpose of the extension, the subject of another competition (but an open one), was the exposition in an accessible manner of the scientific, archaeological, and ethnographic treasures of Scotland in a manner plausible and stimulating to the ordinary visitor. The Alsop scheme, although unplaced in the selection, was a direct precursor of the Swansea scheme. The Scottish treasures were celebrated, enhanced, and made accessible by means of a suspended 'ark' which offered a clear street level gathering-place at which passers-by could experience, and be drawn into, the vaults of the building: valuable relics were housed in a separated and adjacent 'chest' of more conventional construction. The street level space could even be curtained-in for temporary exhibition or festival performances. Although the ark had something of the connotation of a tabernacle, the Word as such stopped short of *tabulae rasae*. Swansea has posed a related set of problems to those solved by the Alsop Edinburgh scheme. As Gooding explains, the key factor about the Word, so to say, is its very invisibility.

In Swansea, Alsop reflected: 'A Museum of the Word is both intriguing and infuriating as a title for the project. Intriguing because it contains all the ambiguity that would permit dreams to become usable – it is infuriating because the very idea of the Word is its invisibility.'

Very soon the whole ensemble of parts that were emerging came to be seen as representative of a multiplicity of means of access to the world of the Word. So this very invisibility of the Word had somehow to be borne out, embraced and celebrated. This process at first involves the display of actual books, accessible microfiches of old and wonderful books, and comprehensive electronic archiving of innumerable books. Provision is made for electronic browsing as it is for real browsing. A Red Box, a Tower of Words, and a Tower of Books seemed to be called for.

Since the Word has its roots in the streets, as the spoken word (as that once was rooted in the glades and groves of an aboriginal Wales), the basic street geography of the immediate city was a prime consideration in generating the building idea. As in Edinburgh, the clearing of the street level space below the ultimate building was vital in allowing key pedestrian routes to intersect and congregate on the site. A pedestrianisation of local streets was already in sway, but terminating meaninglessly at the edge of the site of the Centre. Alsop was determined to create a 'place' or square under the main accommodation of the building, which would in Phase Two incorporate the City Library. So the 'song-lines' of the city memory could be sustained, and developed this way.

The link between the public square and museum and library is the bookshop. It will be possible to ride up in the lifts, visit one or both of the facilities and walk down a gently sloping ramp edged with book shelves, browse and purchase a book at ground level. The design allows the bookshop to maintain independent hours if required. The Glass Box has three levels. The first level contains the Museum of the Word. On leaving the Bookshop (Entrance) a series of suspended forms can be sat in which contain pure light. In such an environment there is a perceived dimension. Inside is received the spoken word (a strong tradition in South Wales). Also in the strip are comfortable chairs with interactive screens. The next strip is a more traditional glass cabinet in which valuable items can be shown. This strip has a glass floor which allows glimpses of its contents to be made from the square below. The following strip contains larger sound environments for words and images. These are contained within fluid spaces. Strip Four is two parallel walls for more conventional display. The space inside can be used as a store if need be. Strip Five contains shelves of books for reference, to-gether with computer terminals, comfortable chairs and domestic quality light. This area is seen as a facilitator to an individual enquiry into the Word. The whole floor is a resource, a resource to be used, a repository for the prose, poetry and matter of Wales.

Alsop incorporates the public library, as Phase Two, in the two floors above the museum. In the interim following construction of Phase One, the 'roof' would be covered with a temporary fabric weather shield. The libraries would be light and spacious, allowing for both air-conditioning and natural (opened windows) ventilation. Fresh air is obtained by means of a 'buffer zone' allowing partial filtering, and so minimising dirt and pollen intrusion. The libraries are to be wholly flexible allowing future restructuring, as well as facilitating peripheral working spaces. Ultimately, the roof of the completed building would be accessible directly for the Bookshop (Entrance). A performance platform and a 'story-telling bush' (a structure to be crawled into), and a roof garden are provided with views out over Swansea, the sea, and the surrounding hills. Alsop has designated the garden as a 'Garden of the World . . . here the idea is to illuminate basic themes of the world – water, fire, skies, animal, earth, etc', as represented in all languages and having a common root. 'The garden is open to the skies and contains some representation of the constellations, stars, moon and sun. We see the whole ensemble as representative of a multiplicity of means of access to the world of the word.'

The Red Box, has specific aims here defined by Mel Gooding. Firstly, to present poetry in such a way as to surprise the casual reader or the non-poetry reader into the recognition that it is a necessity.

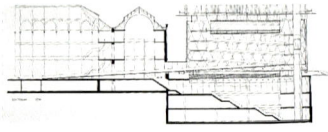

ABOVE: The Museum of Scotland Competition, Edinburgh. The design was a direct source for Swansea in terms of the collaboration of major functional elements of priority within the museum brief: the ground level concourse was open to free pedestrian movement across the site; drop-down screens were employed for the projection of images and for the separation of exhibition areas into identifiable spaces. PREVIOUS PAGE: Conceptual image of the National Writing Centre and City Library, Swansea

There is no culture in human history without poetry, it is the universal expression of things common to all humanity, it is the necessary adjunct to rites of passage. There are poetries of birth, of initiation, of sex, love and marriage, of politics and power, of renunciation, of growing old, of dying, of death.

There are poetries of everyday life: of work; of food and of the getting of food; of survival; of the town and of the country; of the house and of the garden; of rooms; of suffering and of joy. There are poems of occasion and celebration: personal and impersonal; private and public; humble and grand; informal and ceremonial. It is a natural mode of utterance; its rhymes, rhythms and intervals correspond to the naturally ordered recurrences that govern our lives: the beating of the heart, the cycles of waking and sleeping, of day and night; the seasonal turning of the year. Its sounds are musical; poetry is temporal; it has the attributes of tempo, melody, harmony, periodicity, consonance and assonance; its forms are audible, its settings are visual; it has shapes and patterns, its forms are visible. Its formalities may be determined by the impulse to order; its dislocations may reflect disorder. There are poetries of exactitude and poetries of vagueness; poetries of things and poetries of thoughts. It is human utterance at its most 'concise, concentrated and memorable'. 'It is the Promised Land in which language becomes what it really ought to be.' (Calvino).

Secondly, the Red Box aims to demonstrate that poetry is a part of the environment found everywhere: on walls; on gravestones; in memory that can be unlocked; in the words and writings of children; in the rhythms and repetitions of first speech; in dreams; in hymns and popular songs; in books.

This article is concerned primarily with the visionary aspect of Alsop's design for the Centre. Library design, as such, has always imposed special demands upon architects. Whether in the hands of Plecnik at Ljubljana, or Aalto at Viipuri, one of the key tools employed has to be light, and its subtle and dramatic manipulation. This can achieve special significance on entering the building (as in both the historical examples, and with this building especially). Alsop thus draws the library user into a special relationship with the building, unwittingly he or she is propelled upwards. At night too, when the Centre may be busiest, Alsop has cast a magnetic array of lighting across the interior of the building and its elements, hoping to emphasise its key role in the city, as a beacon for the future. And from the roof (as with the Edinburgh project) users can look out over the lights of the city outside.

Alsop has quite possibly advanced the whole concept of a Centre of the Word into a typological revision which will redefine the identity of the genre. If Swansea can be read as a prototype, then in such circumstances the Word and its civilisation connotation becomes, in whatever part of the country or the world, of paramount importance. Alsop's realisable complex of uses might be infinitely reproducible in varying scales of operation.

The physical ramifications of the design are essentially non-contextual. That is the resultant of an inherent universality. But this is, in turn, the product of the very invisibility of the Word. The container receives, stores, dispenses and exchanges the Word. It is also a space to inspire new dreams, visions of many futures. In Wales, the 'dreamtime' has deep roots. Alsop intends to draw them outwards with just that degree of benign sorcery that the age demands.

Conceptual image of the National Writing Centre and City Library, Swansea,

ALSOP & STÖRMER
TY LLEN
Swansea

A response was required which caught the spirit of visionary ambition that had animated Swansea's bid for the title of City of Literature 1995, in the Arts Council *Arts 2000* programme. At the heart of the city's submission was the proposal of a major new building *Ty Llen* (literally, a house of literature). This would be the focal centre for a year of intensive literary activity during the Year of Literature, and following that, the base for a continuing programme into the new millennium. The competition brief was explicit: Swansea expected an architectural statement of international significance.

Aside from the intrinsic enterprise of the undertaking, two aspects of the proposal were of special and immediate significance, each indicative of an uncompromising seriousness of civic intent. The first was the siting of the building at the western end of the commercial centre of the city, opposite the recently renovated Grand Theatre and within the pedestrian ambit of the covered market (one of the liveliest in the UK), the town shopping centre, and the bus station. At the eastern end of this area lie the green spaces around St Mary's, the City Church. *Ty Llen* would not only occupy a central urban site, but one which was of crucial focus within a developing townscape. Secondly, it was proposed to house a new City and County Library within the centre, containing lending, reference and reading sections, and specialist units, such as Arts and Local Studies libraries. The Museum of the Word and the Writers' Centre were to be envisaged not as isolated units but as components of a complex civic, national and international facility. Dedicated to the multivarious uses of language and literature, the facility would be accessible to all people for the diversity of their purposes.

Within the ambitious coherence of the project as a whole, the specifically novel elements are problematic: the concept of the Museum and of the Writers' Centre are in each case incomplete, and it is clear that some part of the process of design will be devoted to the development of ideas and a sharpening of definitions. But in preparing the winning proposal, certain key ideas were instrumental. These had to do as much with the historical and cultural setting of the project, as with the potential forms of the building forms, or with their typologies. *Ty Llen* would be a place of many discourses; a focal centre for the convergence of diverse linguistic energies; a centre for the many activities of language (spoken as well as written); and a place for listening and for reading.

This house of the word is to be built in the centre of a Welsh city, as the centre-place of an international festival – that will be its initial content, at once local, national and international. The Writers' Centre will be of critical importance in this respect: a place to which writers not only from Wales and the United Kingdom, but from all over the world will be invited to work, to discuss their work and give readings from their work, and to print their work. With its comfortable and adaptable interior and its direct, simple and memorable external aspect, the Centre will become an internationally visible *locus*: arbitrarily abstract and uncluttered by reference, it will become an immediately identifiable emblem of the common purpose behind diverse practices in many languages: a forum for intellectual and spiritual exchange.

To fulfil the latter role, the Centre as a whole and the Museum of the Word in particular, must be a place that remembers and celebrates the specific properties of the languages and literatures of Wales itself. By proclaiming its Welsh identity in dynamic relation to the international literary and scholarly community, the Centre will authenticate its function as a sounding chamber for all languages and literatures: there is no universal language but that which lies hidden behind the heterogeneous speech of specific people in local habitations.

Such recollection and celebration must take account of all those branches of Welsh linguistic history in which the spoken and sung word has had primacy: the inspired preaching of the Chapel and the meeting house, taking its cadences and rhythms from the Authorised Version or from the Welsh Bible, heard by generations on a Sunday morning; the poetic rhetoric of radical Welsh politics, the vitalities of its disputation in party rooms and union lodges; the bardic poetries of the eisteddfod; the perfect verbal clarities of great choirs from small villages; the dramatic conorities of Welsh hymns. The design and facilities of the Museum will be developed to reflect this undeniable fact of Welsh cultural and literary history: the sound of the human voice will play a central part in its presentations; not that the Museum and the library above it could neglect the history of the printed work in Wales in its many manifestations – literary, religious, philosophical, political, and academic.

In this respect the Centre in Swansea will occupy a position in a national triangle, in dynamic relation to the National Museum in Cardiff and the National Library in Aberystwyth, and with a line of active connection to the University of Wales, as a valuable resource and as a repository of objects and printed materials. It will not duplicate the facilities and services already provided by those institutions, but create an identity and purpose that complements those that they have established for themselves.

Finally, it is right that the proposal should be for a building that embodies the spirit of festival; a building that is an affirmative act of celebration in a city that has much to commend it as the special site of the Year of Literature. A busy, lively seaside town renewing itself with vision and optimism, deserves a splendid forum, a new landmark. (Swansea has not been well served by its developers and planners since the devastations of war-time bombing.) What could be better at the heart of the town than a brilliant manifestation of the New Modernism: colourful, emblemistic, efficient and economical, democratic in its potential utility; a sociable ensemble of units providing a multiplicity of means of access to the world of the word?

Mel Gooding

MAIN PICTURE: Conceptual image of the Tower of Words; INSET, ABOVE TO BELOW: View of model from the south facade; View of model from the west facade; PREVIOUS PAGE: Conceptual image of the exterior

RICHARD ROGERS
INLAND REVENUE HEADQUARTERS
Nottingham

'The Inland Revenue requires offices which are fit for their purpose and provide value for money. They also seek a building which is in sympathy with the environmental context and enhances it.' In response to this brief, the main concerns of the Richard Rogers Partnership were: to respect the view to and from the castle; to reinforce the landscape of the immediate environment; to create a flexible workplace to absorb change; to produce an environmentally friendly building; and to create a dynamic workplace where a sense of community is promoted.

The most progressive part of their interpretation is an integrated structure and services concept. The strip of land located between the canal and the building enables the shape of the building to derive maximum advantage from the environment. The sealed plenum facade is capable of absorbing noise, deflecting pollution from the railway and controlling the large heat gain element.

Specifically, the design includes louvres on the facade and the atrium and the tapered edge of slab which reduce the glare and diffuse daylight deep into offices. Air extraction by stack effect via the atrium, negates the conventional requirement for suspended ceilings. A thermal mass of the exposed structural soffit contributes to the cooling cycle of the building. Personal control through individual task lighting and by opening windows affords local temperature variation. A roof system performing a passive role as reservoir of hot air increases the stack effect, replacing mechanical extraction.

The temperate environment of the UK lends itself well to the concept of passive environmental control. This low energy system seeks primarily to capitalise on the temperate nature of the average UK day with a mix-mode heating and cooling system that limits its major mechanical interventions to periods of troughs and peaks. In this way, whilst the building systems have the capacity to react mechanically when needed (peak and trough periods), normal operation is limited to the manipulation of external air to ensure the comfort of the workforce. The resultant yearly internal temperature variation

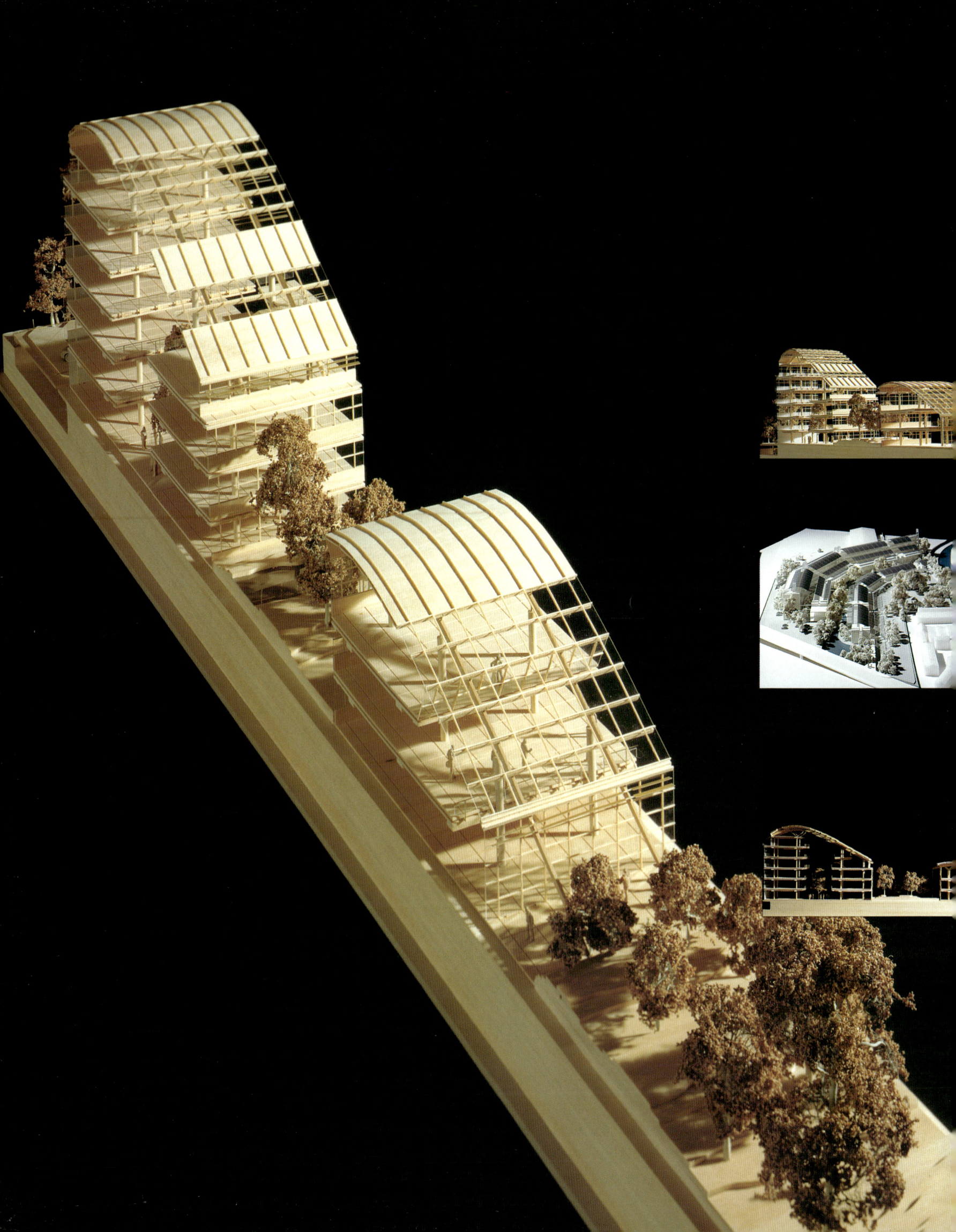

illustrates greater perception of seasonal fluctuations which is the hallmark of an environmentally friendly building.

Computer modelling was developed to monitor the thermal performance and consequent energy consumption at representative periods through a given year in order to identify hot spots and design out problems before construction.

Low energy building servicing systems rely on orientation to reduce unwanted heat gain/loss and on tapping into free sources of energy and light. These sources of energy are used in varying densities to control internal thermal comfort. During the majority of the year most areas of the building rely on fresh air from open windows; the southern offices with the sealed skin rely on the plenum system for fresh air. To keep the building cool it is sufficient to use free night time cooling of the structure to maintain daytime comfort. However, during peak summertime some mechanical cooling will be required. Cooling will be by heat exchange with water and not by mechanical refrigeration plant. To heat the building during the winter, all areas have a conditioned fresh air supply heated by solar energy and heat recovery. Free heating can be provided by condensing boilers used in combination with combined heat power units, generating free heat whilst producing electricity.

Passive environmental control considerably reduces the running cost, the capital cost and generally provides a more comfortable and marketable building. The interior space is designed to be aesthetically pleasing and conducive to work. Every element works towards the same environmental principle.

Architects: Laurie Abbott, Mark Darbon, Michael Davies, James Finestone, Stuart Forbes-Waller, Marco Goldschmied, Philip Gumuchdjian, John Lowe, Louise Pritchard, Kim Quasi, Richard Rogers, Stephen Spence, Andrew Tyley, Chris Wan, John Young; Structural Engineers: OAP – Alistair Lechner; Service Engineers: OAP – Guy Battle and Andy Sedgewick; Quantity Surveyor: Turner Townsend

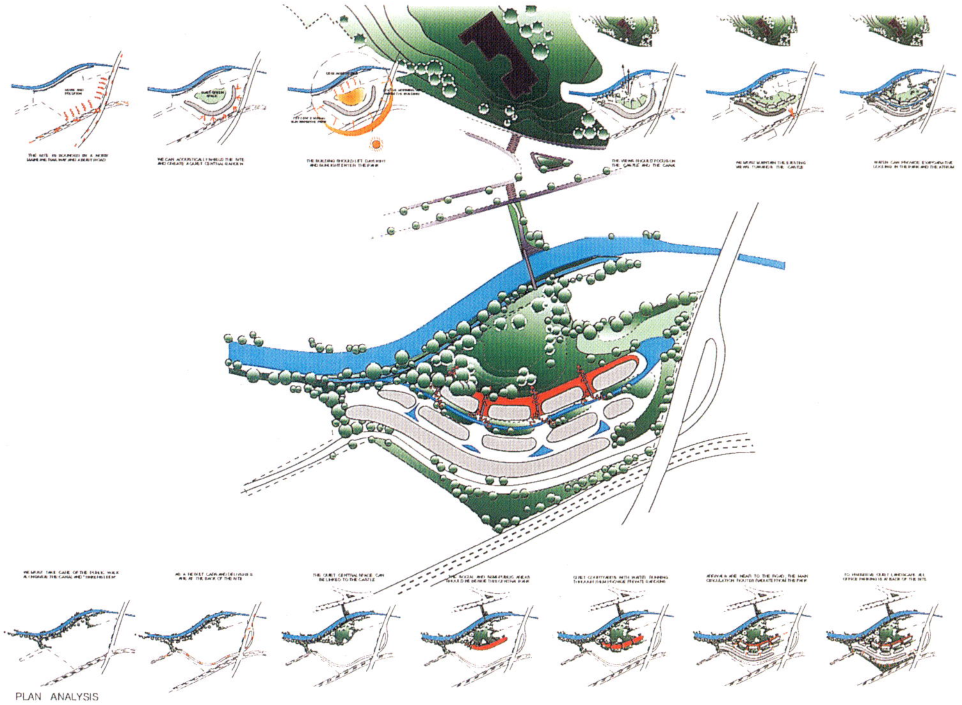

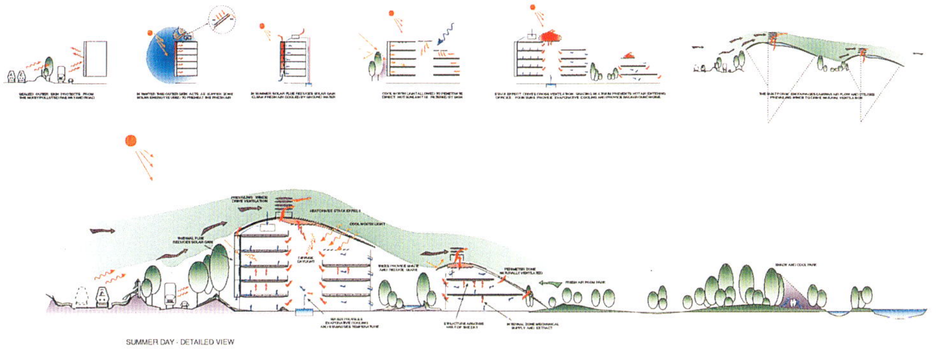

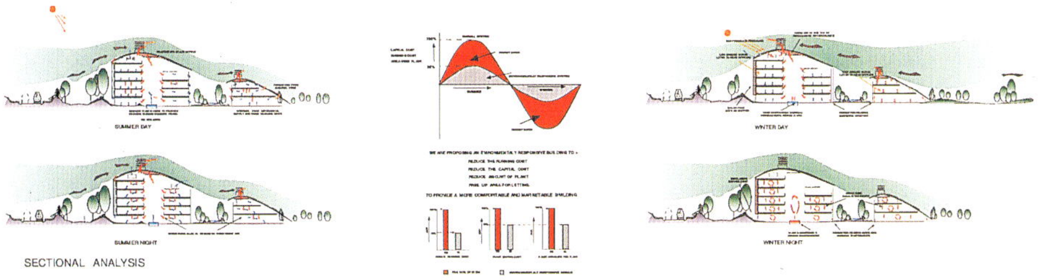

ABOVE: Site plan; CENTRE: Section; BELOW: Perspective view; OPPOSITE: View of sectional model; INSET, ABOVE TO BELOW: Views of model; PREVIOUS PAGE: Sectional model indicating positioning of floor and roof

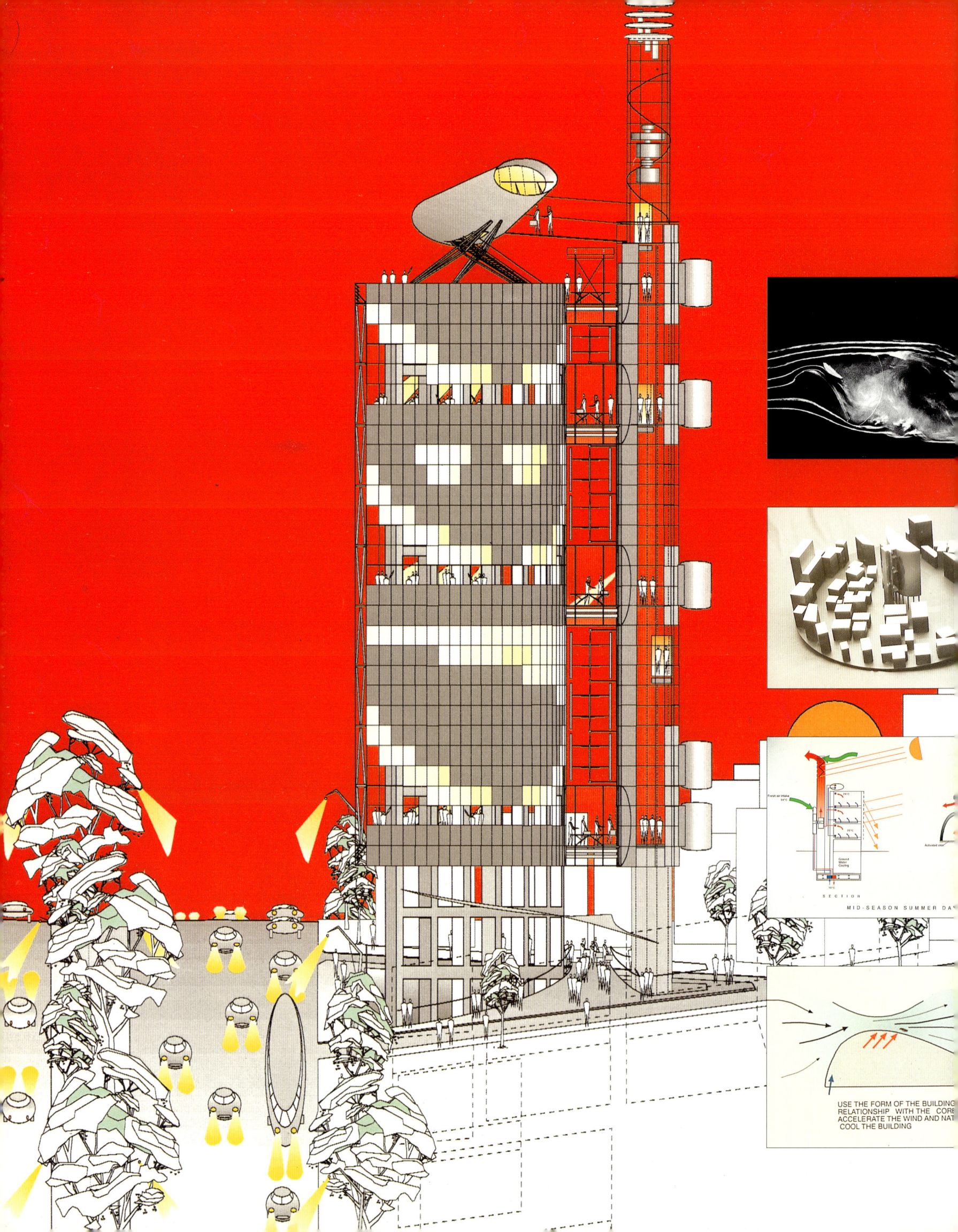

TOMIGAYA II
Tokyo, Japan

The Tomigaya project is situated on a triangular area of a small hill overlooking Yoyogi Park in Central Tokyo. The unusually high planning restrictions in this area allow for a very tall building which emphasises the elegance, drama and impact of the design. The heavy concrete structure is exposed to absorb heat and moderate the internal environment. The core is separated from the main building block and the building is smooth and shaped to encourage the wind to pass through the gap in the building. The service tower to the north of the building, works as a chimney under the action of the sun and wind to help extract hot stale air. The northern facade is patterned with clear glass, diffused glass and opaque panels to allow views and light to enter where needed whilst insulating elsewhere. The southern facade, which is fully glazed as a client requirement, has a variable shading system that is turned according to the time of day, the season and whether the sun is shining. Water around the deep basement is used to provide peak summer cooling and to warm cool air during the winter.

Tomigaya is designed as a total energy system within which each element is tuned to achieve low running costs. By reducing the necessary plant, the lettable area which contributes to the clients revenue is increased. The scheme has intelligent reactive facades that change like a chameleon to provide a cool comfortable internal environment.

The building form is modelled to compress and accelerate the prevailing winds to pass between the main building and its service core, to drive a wind turbine to provide power. Measurements of wind velocity from 360 degrees of wind direction have shown that an increase in wind speed of over two times can be expected. This is reinforced by flow visualisation using smoke, which shows that enhanced flow passes through the gap for at least two thirds of the total 360 degree wind. Calculations based on a reasonable turbine efficiency of 50% and estimates of the mean wind speed and shear at the side, indicate that the turbines would generate in the order of 55 kilowatts per hour – more than is sufficient to service the building as well as providing some of its small power. Energy is used directly when possible and excess is stored on site or supplied into the main grid. The project itself demonstrates a process of design that leads to a more holistic architectural solution.

The design recognises the fundamental connection between culture, climate and comfort. Tokyo's hot humid summers and noisy and polluted roads, demand efficient cooling systems and prohibit the direct use of fresh air without some form of filtering system. The fabric of the building is tuned to respond to the site and the orientation and use within. The rear passive facade has fixed apertures that are set out so that they permit a fixed solar gain across the whole floor while the southern facade has a variable shading system. The shades are contained within a double solar flue that not only effectively controls the solar gain, but also acts as an efficient acoustic barrier.

The initial results show that it is possible to make the Tomigaya project 100% self sufficient in terms of energy production. Significant savings in energy can only be achieved if the design team has a clear understanding of the environmental opportunities presented by a project, right from the initial stages.

As legislation and need focus attention on the requirement to save energy, buildings will be forced to respond suit. As this need increases, so will the influence of the environment on the form and shape of architecture in the future.

Architects: Laurie Abbott, Mike Davies, Marco Goldschmied, Richard Rogers, Andrew Wright, John Young; Structural Engineers: OAP – Chris McCarthy Service Engineers: OAP – Guy Battle and Chris Twinn; Other: Aeronautics Imperial College – Professor Mike Graham

RIGHT: Sketch; OPPOSITE: Elevation; INSET, ABOVE TO BELOW: Wind tunnel – winter wind; Model; Theory of temperature control; Wind theory

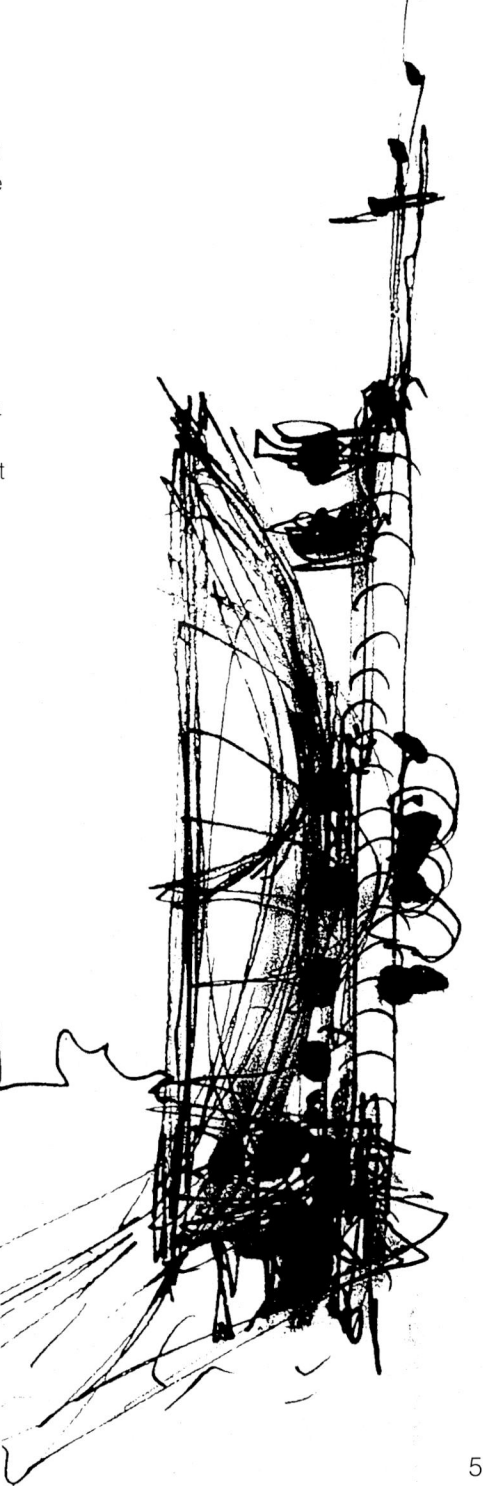

LU JIA ZUI, SHANGHAI, CHINA
A Vision of the City of the Future

Urban design proposals for the western part of the district of Shanghai called Lu Jia Zui, have been developed by the Richard Rogers Partnership in conjunction with the Ove Arup Partnership, the Bartlett school of Architecture Unit for Architectural Research and Cambridge Architectural Research in response to the brief prepared by Shanghai Lu Jia Zui Central Area International Planning and Urban Design Consultation Committee. This is their vision for a City of the Future . . .

In order to ensure that the design for Lu Jia Zui in Shanghai accommodates the changes that will inevitably occur over the time lapse between planning and realisation, flexibility has been incorporated into the design. The development of the plan will be accompanied by the development of a computer software system that allows an analytical appraisal of changes in population, parking energy balance and movements of people etc. This system would generate design drawings from numeric data gleaned from five major research areas: the links to the Shanghai CBD and Pu Dong; the transportation network; the city parks; the network of secondary public spaces and the street layout. The results are transposed into a three-dimensional visualisation of an urban space or resources distribution pattern. For example, actual traffic levels or pedestrian movements in public spaces could be modelled, light levels at various times of the day within a building or in a public space predicted and so on.

Another innovation is the integration of disciplines such as traffic engineers, transportation, specialists in the design of public spaces, computer programmers, environmental geographers, wind specialists and service engineers. The software ensures that the conclusions from each of these independent studies are amalgamated to allow proper recognition of the impact of one set of decisions on another.

A co-ordinated energy strategy is planned where the energy requirements of seven different types of buildings have been calculated: offices, housing, hotels, conference, shopping, cultural and leisure centres. The area has been split into six zones. The building types have been split amongst the zones to give an even mix of space coverage, energy use and compatible uses. One energy centre will provide the energy for two zones. The energy required has been split between thermal energy – required for heating, energy required for cooling and electrical energy for lighting etc. Energy use standards have been proposed to ensure that buildings are energy efficient with good thermal properties and energy saving controls. The total energy required for the development area, if energy efficient buildings were built, would be 135MW. This is divided between 61MW for heating, 14MW for cooling and 60MW of electricity generation.

The building massing has been designed to ensure maximum daylight and views over the Huang Pu River and to the Bund. This has been achieved by expressing collected data on a graph and a contour drawing. By examining the wave-like profile with peaks and troughs and overlapping waves, optimum massing can be realised: the inner ring of development is designed as dense clusters of buildings and the outer ring undulates to maintain the views. To maximise the daylight admitted to the building, a model was made and tested for both summertime and wintertime conditions. Lighting of buildings typically consumes 30 per cent of the total energy used by buildings. Maximising daylight admission to building can reduce dependence on artificial lighting. This results in approximately 15 per cent savings in energy costs.

The focus of the project is a large central park which, with the linear park proposed in the master plan by the Municipality of Shanghai, will mean that green space will be located at the heart and at the perimeter of the development. All areas of Lu Jia Zui will be within easy reach of open space.

The commercial development (offices, hotels etc) will be focused along the light rail loop. Cultural and social facilities are concentrated around the open spaces. Housing is clustered at the sub-centre and shopping is located along the primary routes leading to the river crossing. This strategy achieves a good mix of activities within each of the six sectors of the city and a balance between commercial and residential activities which evens out demands on the infrastructure: for example, power generation, transport etc. The buildings that line the Bund create a skyline that is famous and has been frequently represented in paintings and photographs. However it is of a 19th-century scale. The skyline of Lu Jia Zui will be of a larger scale appropriate to a city of the 21st century. The two should respect each other.

The transport plan is designed as a co-ordinated network that structures the Development Zone. It proposes that each sector is centred on a light rail station with an associated parking structure for 2,500 cars. A circular feeder road runs along the inner edge of the development zone giving access to the parking structures. Vehicle access beyond these roads is restricted to taxis, bicycles, buses and delivery vehicles. No street will be pedestrianised. The light rail system is the most significant element in the public transportation network. It forms a circular loop through the centre of the development zone. Operating requirements of the light rail system define the ideal distance between stations (600 metres). Four of the six stations coincide with subway connections. The light rail is supplemented by a tram route around the outer edge of the development zone which allows for a maximum walking distance of 350 metres.

Architects: Laurie Abbott, Hal Curry, Mike Davies, Marco Goldschmied, Richard Rogers, Simon Smithson, John Young, Andrew Wright; Service Engineers: OAP – Guy Battle, Alan Mason (Traffic), Susan Freed

OPPOSITE: Model of masterplan; INSET, ABOVE TO BELOW: Computer originated views (x2); Plan showing layout of development areas and open spaces; Site plan showing links to Shanghai Central Business District and Pu Dong

NORMAN FOSTER AND PARTNERS
CRANFIELD LIBRARY
Bedfordshire

The new library at Cranfield Institute of Technology was opened in October 1992. It unites two existing library collections and also serves as an information technology centre. It provides a 180-seat lecture theatre and three seminar rooms. The building has been designed to adapt easily in the future to information technology advances. Library users have access to on-line connections to computer networks and electronic databases. Students can plug in personal computers or lap-tops with instant access to the Institute's network.

The library consists of four lightweight steel vaulted roof forms; one forms an atrium linking all three floors, becoming the focus of the library. The external walls are a clear glass curtain which give views into the library study areas. The overhanging roof provides sheltered walkways along the side of the building creating an entrance canopy. An external screen of silver anodised aluminium louvres provides shading.

One of the prime design criteria was durability and low maintenance. The library has all glass facades, fairfaced block internal walls with ceramic skirting blocks, stainless steel door jams, skirtings to partitions, and fairfaced concrete. Careful shading design minimises the external heat gains during the summer months and allows comfort conditions to be maintained through a ventilation only system. Future flexibility has been designed into the main library ventilation system to allow the use of direct-expansion cooling plant to restrict peak temperatures, should the information technology infrastructure be utilised fully. The furniture system has been designed by Norman and Sabiha Foster.

Service Engineers: J Roger Preston & Partners; Structural Engineers: Ove Arup & Partners.

ABOVE TO BELOW: Cross section; Longitudinal section; Ground floor plan; OPPOSITE: Detail of facade; INSET, ABOVE TO BELOW: Entrance canopy and glass facade; Interior; External screen with aluminium louvres; Exterior at night; OVERLEAF: Exterior at night

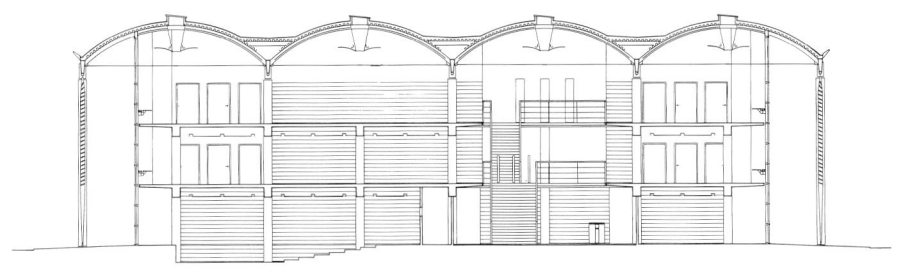
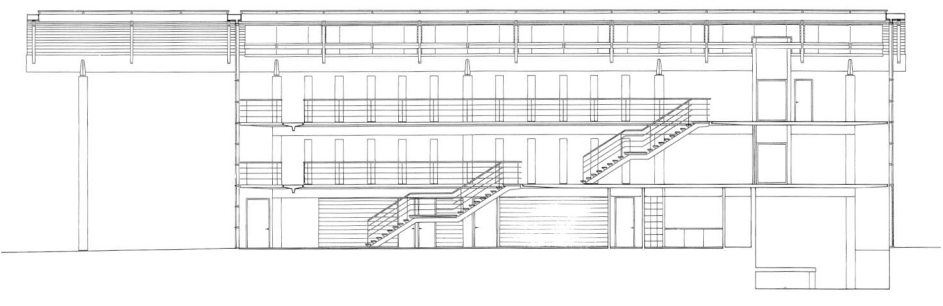
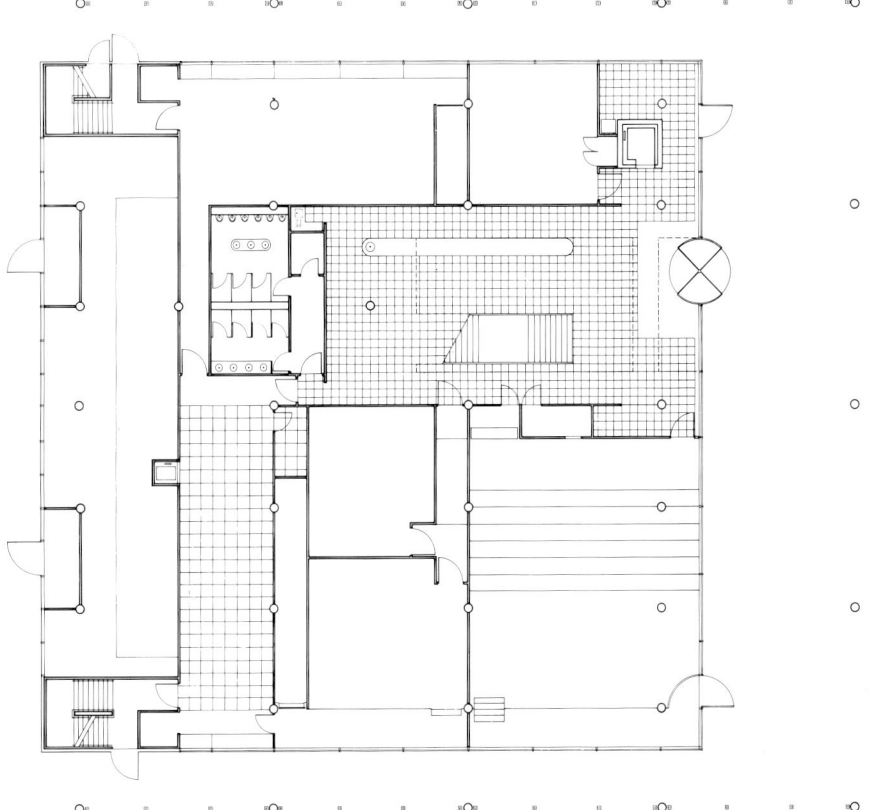

DUISBURG
Micro Electronics Park, Neudorf

The Micro Electronics Park consists of the Business Promotion Centre, the Telematic Centre and the Micro Centre. The project is sited in Neudorf on the main axis road between the city centre and the University. The Business Promotion Centre is an eight-storey building with an underground car park and a total area of 4,000m². Its purpose is to act as a landmark, representing the will for social and structural change in the Ruhr area. Consequently, the tenants will be selected companies promoting economy and helping start-ups and spin-offs. There is a banking and exhibition hall in a double height space on the ground floor. The rest of the building is filled with a mixture of cellular offices and meeting spaces. The top three floors terrace upwards to allow for promotional spaces with a possibility for public usage.

The cladding is a layered system. The outer skin is of Pilkington Planar glazing; the middle layer is the cavity with computer controlled blinds; and the inner layer, or back-up wall, consists of transparent insulation material from Kaiser Bautechnik. The inner layer insulates and moderates the building and its occupants from extremes of outside temperature and provides a better overall degree of comfort for the building's users. The building is air conditioned with a source flow fresh air supply and radiant (water) cooling in the suspended ceiling. The hot and cold water will be produced by thermally powered absorption coolers. The Telematic Centre has started on site and is located in a residential area. The building is an extension of the existing Technology Transfer Centre (GTT) with a total area of 3,500m².

This building will have a seven metre high multi-functional computer market/exhibition space underground and will rise five storeys above ground. An atrium of approximately 12 metres wide, runs through the building, broadening at the base. The

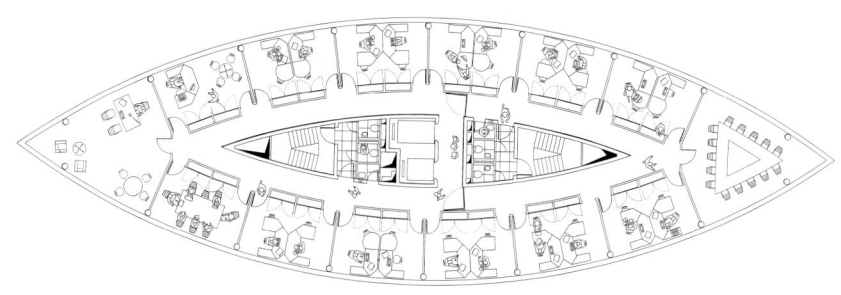

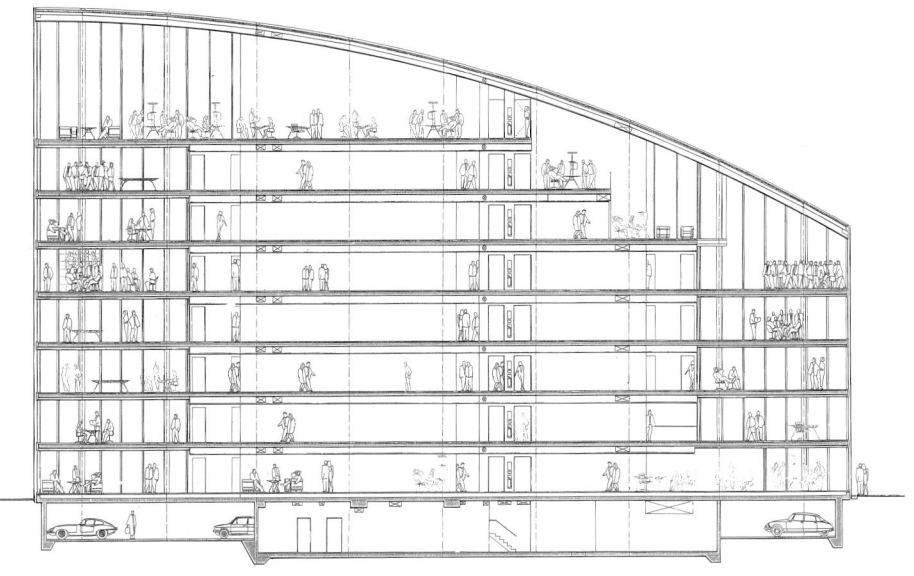

Business Promotion Centre ABOVE: Cross section; CENTRE: Typical floor plan; BELOW: Longitudinal section; OPPOSITE: View of model

underground station provides an exhibition space, catering for electronic and video conference facilities, video and database workshop rooms and lecture rooms. All utility technical services and the Building Management system are monitored and controlled by direct digital control (DDC) systems. The Telematic Centre will be the centre or brain for this system. Both the Business Promotion Centre and the Micro Centre's building management system will be linked to the Telematic Centre, providing all occupants with access to the most advanced telecommunications facilities including ISDN, electronic mail and international video conferences.

The Micro Centre is set in a residential area and stretches across Bismarkstrasse. In the Foster Associates original masterplan of 1988, it was stated that half the site should become a new public park next to the building, the approximate area of which was 30,000m². The project consists of 12 building blocks grouped under two climate halls. The individual units will have a maximum of five storeys above ground and the outer building envelope will be 22 metres high, with an underground car park.

The purpose of the building is to create ideal working conditions and flexibility for a wide range of micro-electronics related companies. Modern production spaces, laboratories and workshops suitable for the special requirements of micro-electronic production have been provided. The climate halls will create a micro-climate allowing semi-public and public activities around and above the individual building blocks throughout the year. The individual blocks will contain both cellular and open plan offices. The external envelope uses transparent insulation material, special light-guiding systems (for example holograms), sun reflectors and heat collectors to create the optimum temperature balance and gain, depending on outside climate conditions. Air conditioning is achieved by employing air intake ducts located in the park, pulling the air through underground pipes; thereby taking advantage of the earth's constant temperature for primary cooling and heating. Additionally, the water pool along the length of the building will be used for heat exchange and storage.

Structural Engineer: Ingenieur büro Dr Meyer

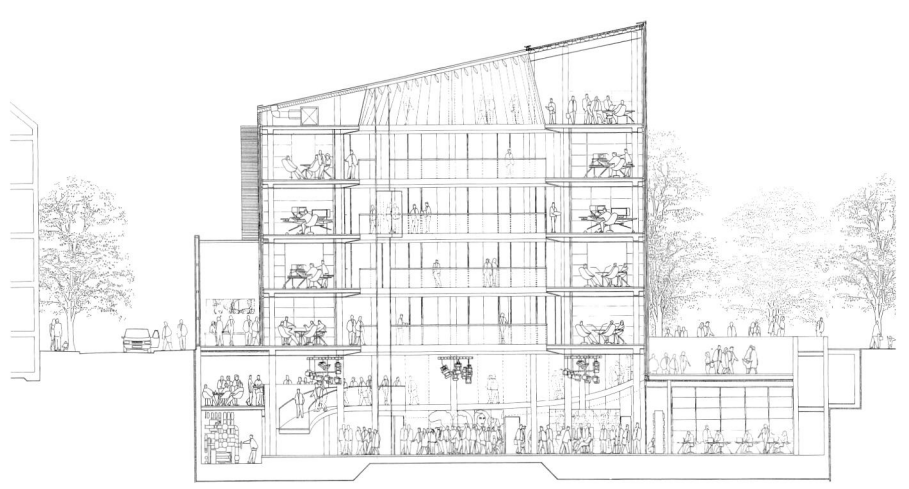

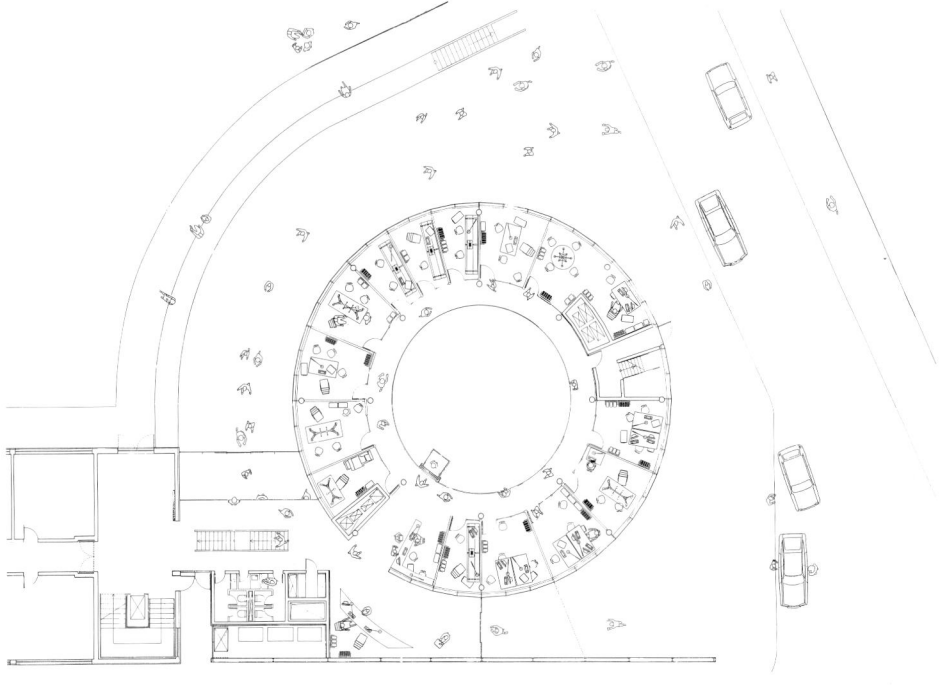

Telematic Centre ABOVE: Longtitudinal section; BELOW: Ground floor plan; OPPOSITE: Model

VON GERKAN, MARG AND PARTNERS
PASSENGER TERMINAL
Stuttgart Airport

The new terminal is reduced to two elementary forms: a long section on a triangular cross section and a rectangular hall on a trapezoid cross section. These geometric shapes provide the focal points that put some order into the heterogeneous environment of the present airport.

The roof rises from the road access side towards the runways, in an indirect symbolic expression of the concepts 'gate' and 'flying'. More directly, the construction of the terminal roof is based on the structure of a tree, thus providing an unmistakeable and individual feature for Stuttgart Airport.

Where the aircraft park, the departure lounges and routes between the road and flight sides are arranged in a long building. Its base has a cross section resembling a dike because of the difference in height of the terrain on either side. So the building perches as if on the ridge of a hill, also acting as a noise barrier between the runways and the surrounding area. The terminal hall, covered only by the tree-structure of the roof, is open on all sides.

At the front, the two elements of the building overlap and intersect. The spine of the long building ends in the hall in terraces, which project in arching semi-circles in the centre. The VIP lounge, conference rooms, and the observation terrace lie on the 'ridge' of the spine.

The base of the building is clad in natural stone and so rustication is an essential feature. The windows are recessed and stand vertical in the oblique plane, creating a strong plastic effect over the monolithic base, with the openwork steel construction rising above it. The wall of the terminal building faces south and is fully glazed; it has blinds with rotating wing-like sections, which operate automatically to provide different degrees of shading.

Design: Meinhard von Gerkan, Karsten Brauer, Klaus Staratzke

ABOVE TO BELOW: North elevation; South elevation; Cross section; Site plan; OPPOSITE: South facade; INSET, ABOVE TO BELOW: View from the North-east; Tree structure; Ventilation system; South facade; OVERLEAF: Interior

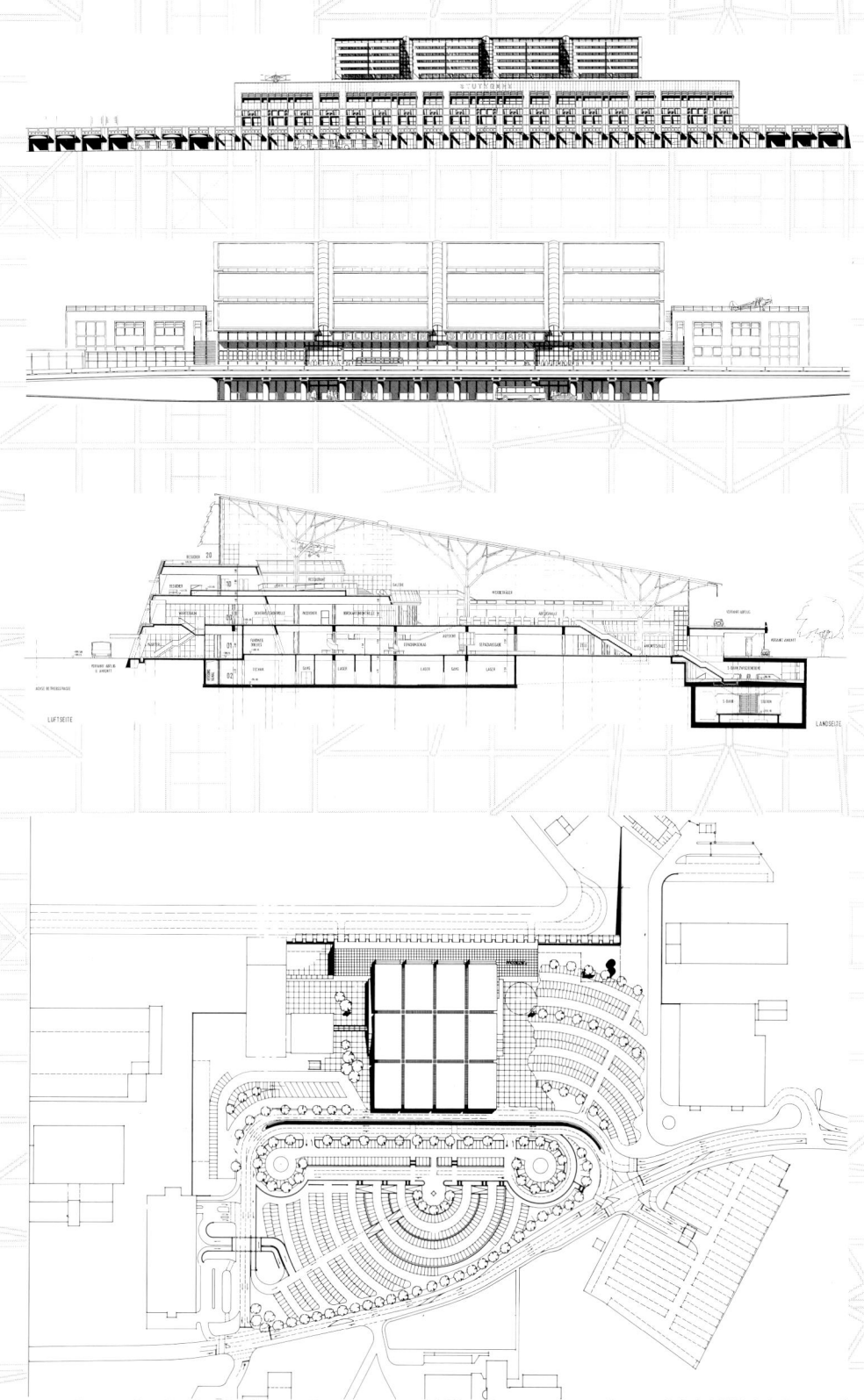

CITY RAIL STOP
Bielefeld

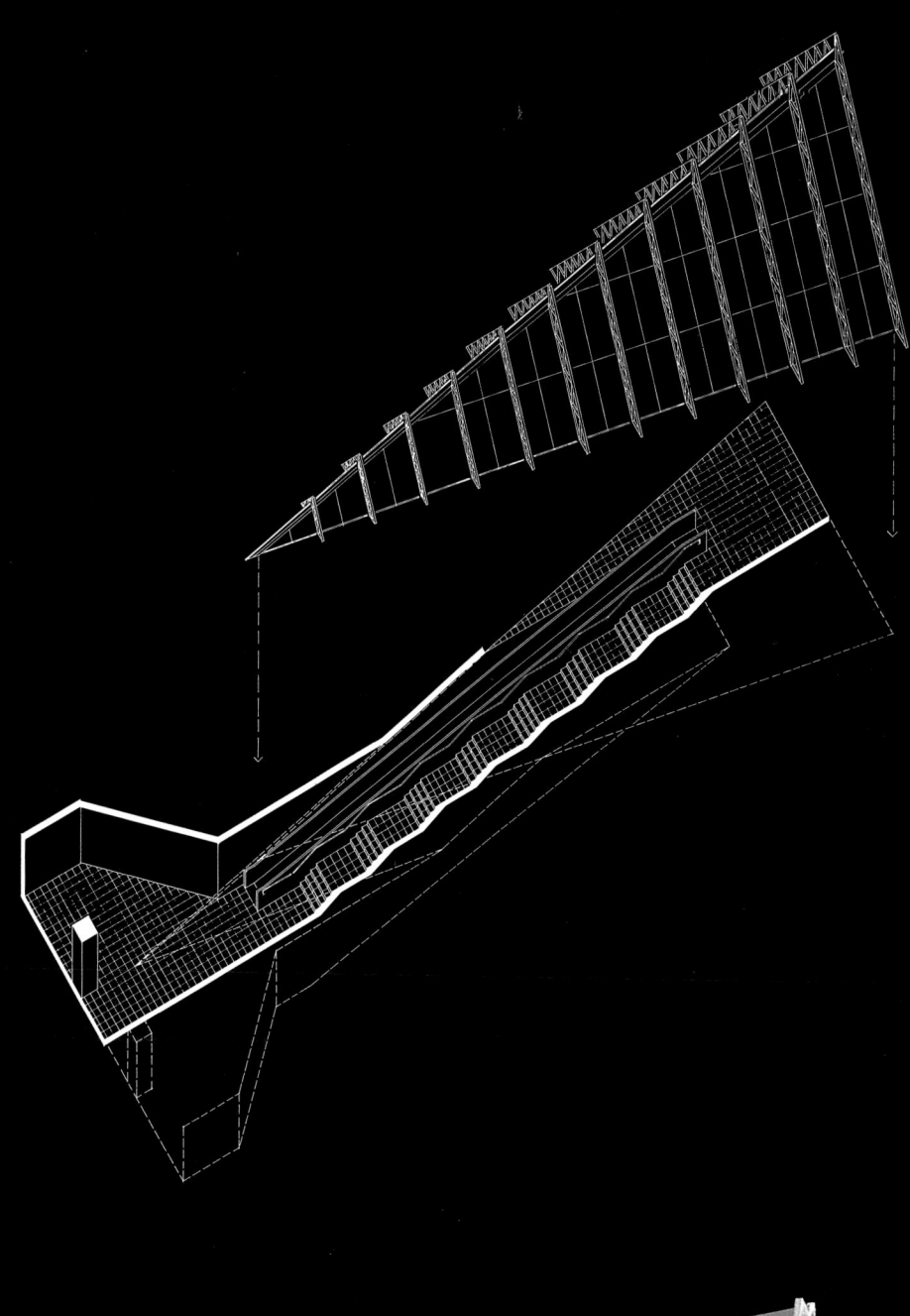

The main feature of the design of the station is the use of light. The skilful placing of the platform lights, which were developed specifically for this railway station, ensures that the platforms are brightly lit. The roof and the tracks remain dark. This creates linear areas of light that offer a new quality of spatial experience through the sequence of light and dark. The access area, an area 30 metres wide and 35 metres long, without roof supports, was required. For structural reasons the height could only be 2.85 metres. This is too low for the area but the use of indirect lighting raises the height visually. The reflection of the lighting in a mirrored roof above the lights gives the impression that the source of light is floating above the roof. The roof cloud floats over the high frontage of the access area linking it with the platform level, thus giving the area its own dynamic plasticity. This motif is applied to the wall areas, too, where it also serves to identify the platform levels.

The need to make the city rail stop visible from the railway station gave rise to the idea of a ramp-like connection between the road and the stop. The transparency of the building, the opening up of the lower ground level and the glass prism above ground with a view directly onto it, make the stop clearly visible from a distance.

Design: Meinhard von Gerkan with Hans-Heinrich Möller

ABOVE: Isometric; BELOW: Model of roof/entrance; OPPOSITE: Perspective view of roof/entrance; INSET, ABOVE TO BELOW: Views of roof/entrance of station (x2); Interior

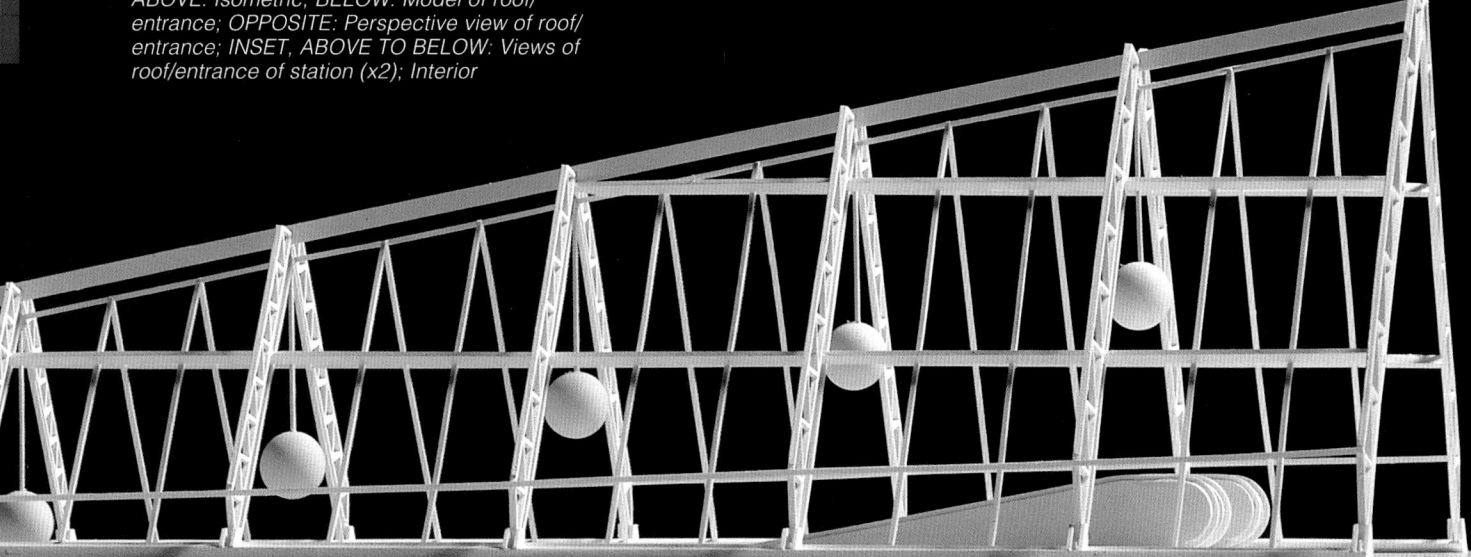

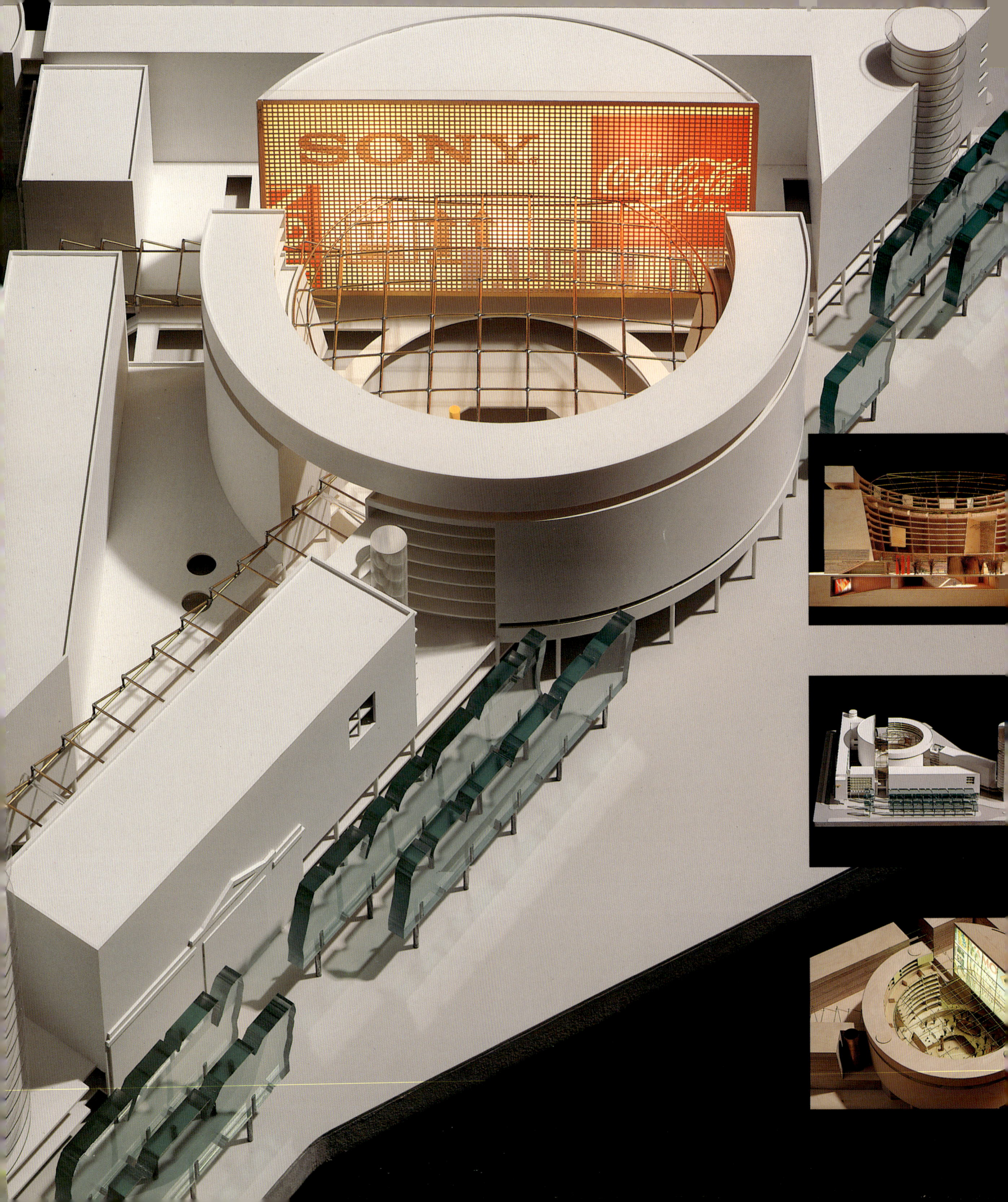

SONY BERLIN GMBH
Potsdamer Platz, Berlin

The aim of the design concept was to create an urban area to enhance metropolitan life in a place with a very special quality of life. Although the triangular shape of the building site may appear disadvantageous, it will meet all the requirements if the concept is adapted to the particular conditions of the site and creates a form with a unique and unmistakeable identity.

The triangular site has urban areas of a completely different character on each of its three sides. To the south and east, are the new Potsdamer Strasse and the Potsdamer Platz with their bustling life, pulsating traffic, bus stops, public transport, shops, restaurants, malls and office buildings. To the north-east are the parklike greens of the Tiergarten, functioning as a place of relaxation, and to the west is the Kulturforum with the Philharmonie, Staatsbibliothek and several museums.

Three aspects of urban life – business and shopping, rest and relaxation, and cultural activities – are linked together by the design, both spatially and architecturally, with the Sony site as the main focus.

The circular inner space, 55 metres in diameter, will provide a setting for all urban activities. An almost completely transparent glass roof protects dozens of shops, boutiques, restaurants and cafes.

Competition: Award, 1992
Assistants: Kai Voss,
Jens Kalkbrenner

RIGHT: Site plan; OPPOSITE: Model views

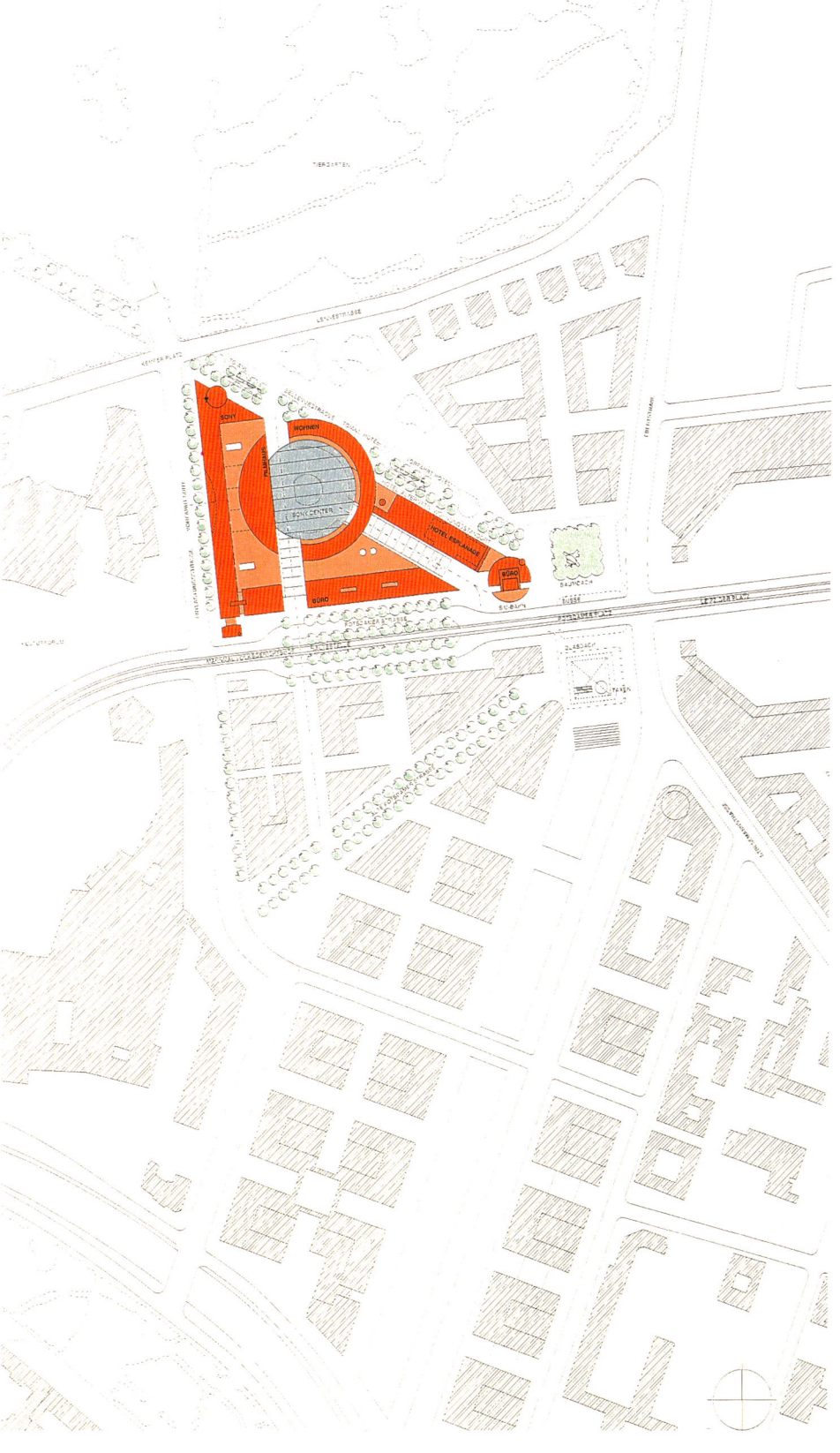

SANTIAGO CALATRAVA
LYON AIRPORT RAILWAY STATION
Lyon, France

There is no such thing as a straight line in nature, so the curve comes quite naturally to Santiago Calatrava. He will give any function a shape. He doesn't create a curve to catch the eye. He breathes life into design and does not conform to the intellectually acquired process that stifles modern architecture. Beauty exists on the borderline of tangible and ethereal, on the borderline between the temporal and the casual world. It is an echo of the one source that we cannot otherwise grasp.

This scheme is probably larger and more complex than any other of Calatrava's realised projects. Despite its daunting size, the station is essentially a monumental magnification of earlier roof and pavilion forms. The six tracks are enclosed by a 500 metre long, shallow vaulted structure which stretches out along the platforms, crisscrossed with a lattice arrangement of concrete ribs. The station hall (as yet unbuilt) is reminiscent of a huge bird of prey wrestling with its victim; wings outstretched it is positioned in the centre of the platform vault. From the north elevation of this section you can see the taut curve demonstrating Calatrava's sculptural inspiration.

The station has been conceived to connect the high speed train network, which will eventually run between Paris and Marseilles to Lyon Airport.

RIGHT: Ground plan; OPPOSITE: Detail of concrete structure

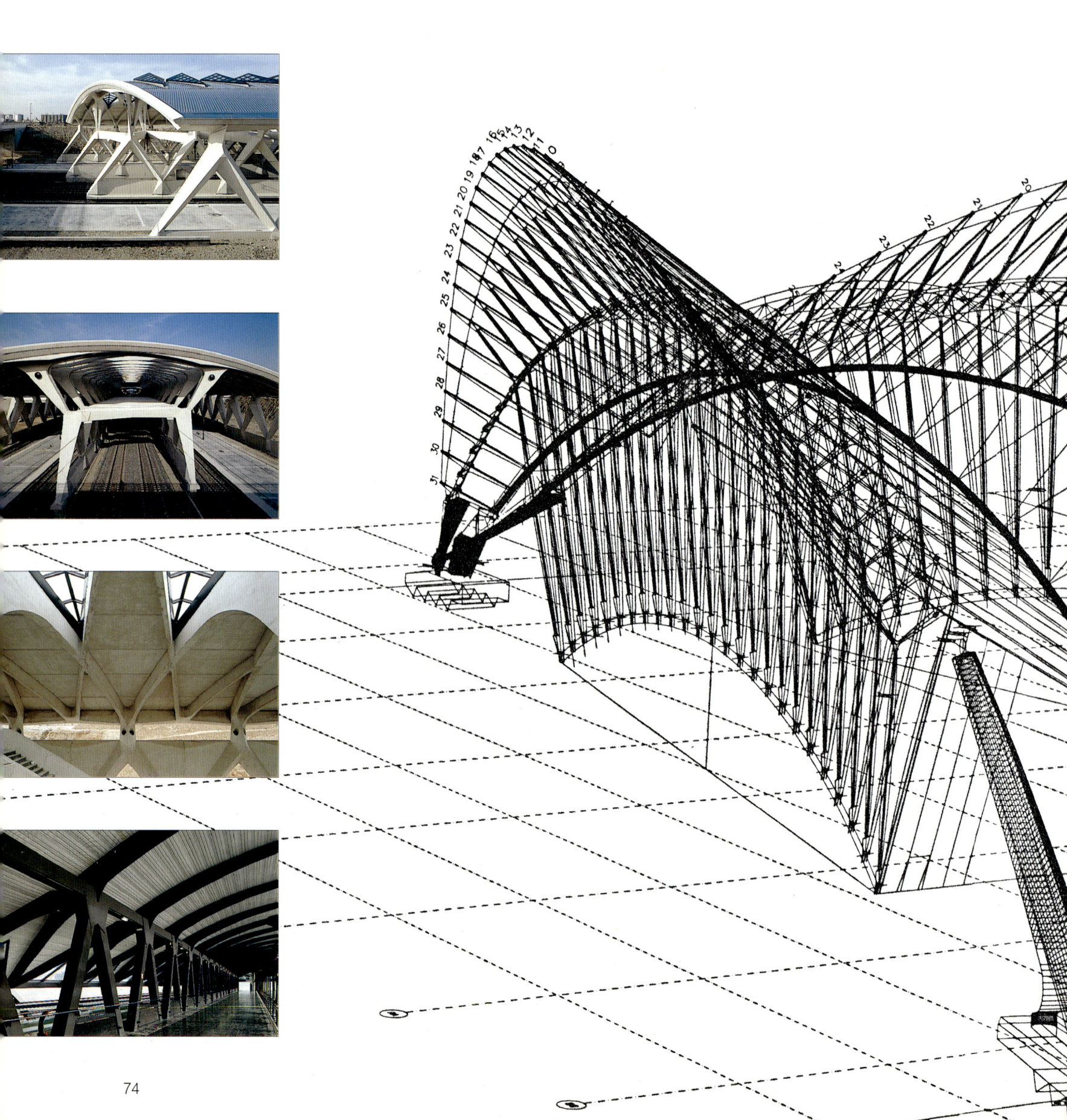

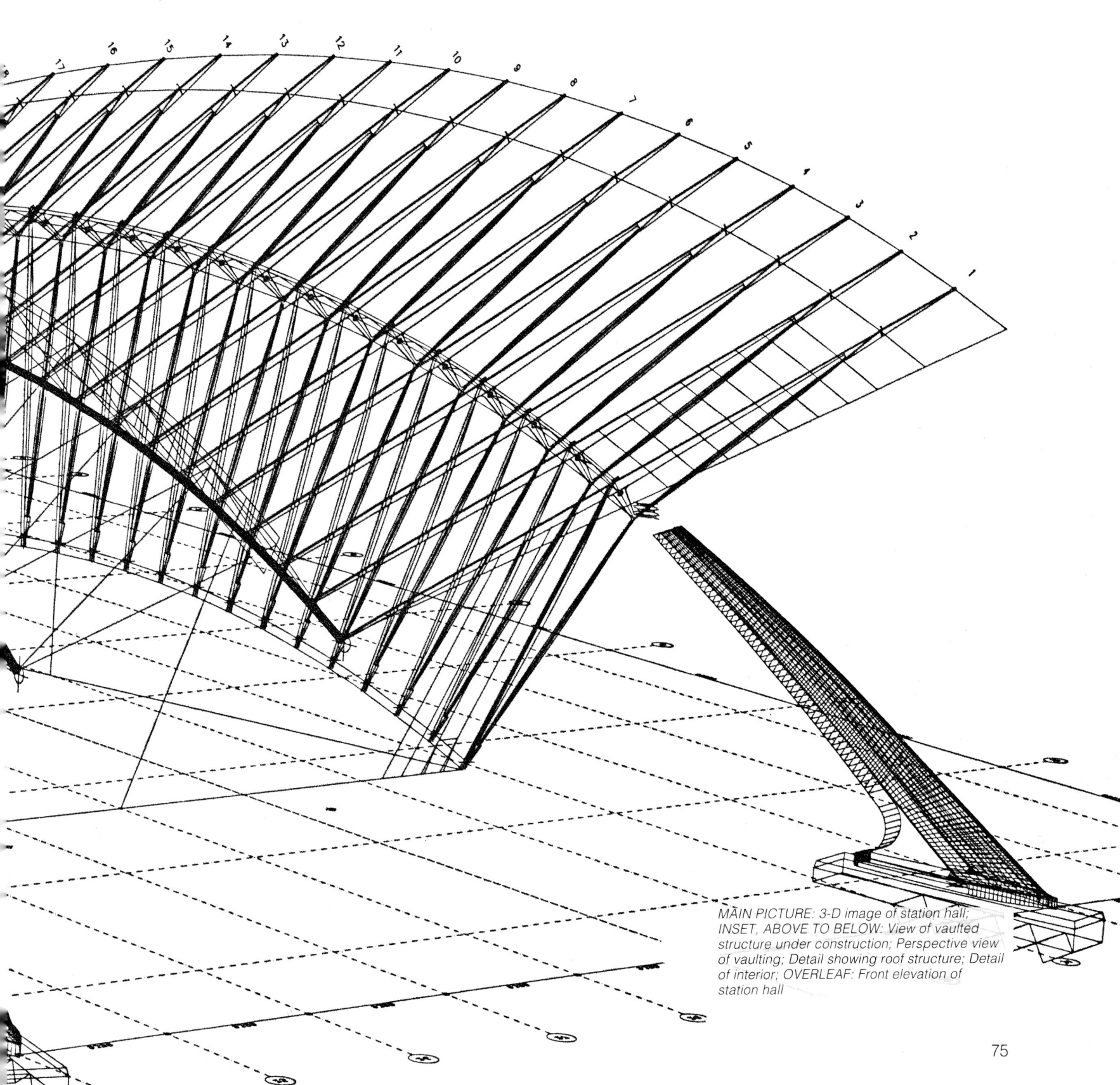

MAIN PICTURE: 3-D image of station hall; INSET, ABOVE TO BELOW: View of vaulted structure under construction; Perspective view of vaulting; Detail showing roof structure; Detail of interior; OVERLEAF: Front elevation of station hall

FUTURE SYSTEMS
GREEN BUILDING
London

Developers of modern office buildings have created a working environment which is closely controlled to nullify external modulating influences and which rely on complex interventional systems to achieve this degree of containment, using large amounts of energy. The purpose of the Green Building project has been to examine a number of strategies and techniques for achieving an alternative office environment – an environment that is controlled directly by the occupants and not by automatic machines. In architecture there is always an expectation that ideas should be expressed in a concrete form. Here a conceptual building has been created from the explorations and experiments undertaken, but this is really only a beginning. The objective was not to seek to alter the skyline of London but rather to influence a way of thinking. The triangular site is in the centre of the City of London, a dense and urban site typical of the area. The entire building is effectively supported by a giant tripod megastructure. The tripod legs, constructed using similar technology to the tubular steel legs of an oil platform, have cigar-like profiles to optimise the distribution of material for bending strength and overall stability. The weight of all the floors and the facades is supported from the apex of the tripod by a system of suspension ties which pick up the floor plates at intervals around their internal and external edges. By analogy the gravity support principle for the floors could be considered similar to the support of the hoops in a hooped dress. The lateral loads due to wind are supported directly at each floor by the bending strength of the tripod legs. Overall horizontal stability is assured by the tripod's triangulation.

The floor decks are constructed as hollow steel boxes stiffened internally by web plates in a similar way to the deck of a modern suspension bridge. The external skin enveloping the building is supported from the edge of the floors at each level by a system of props and ties which also space the facade from the floors to allow for natural ventilation. A network of ties braces

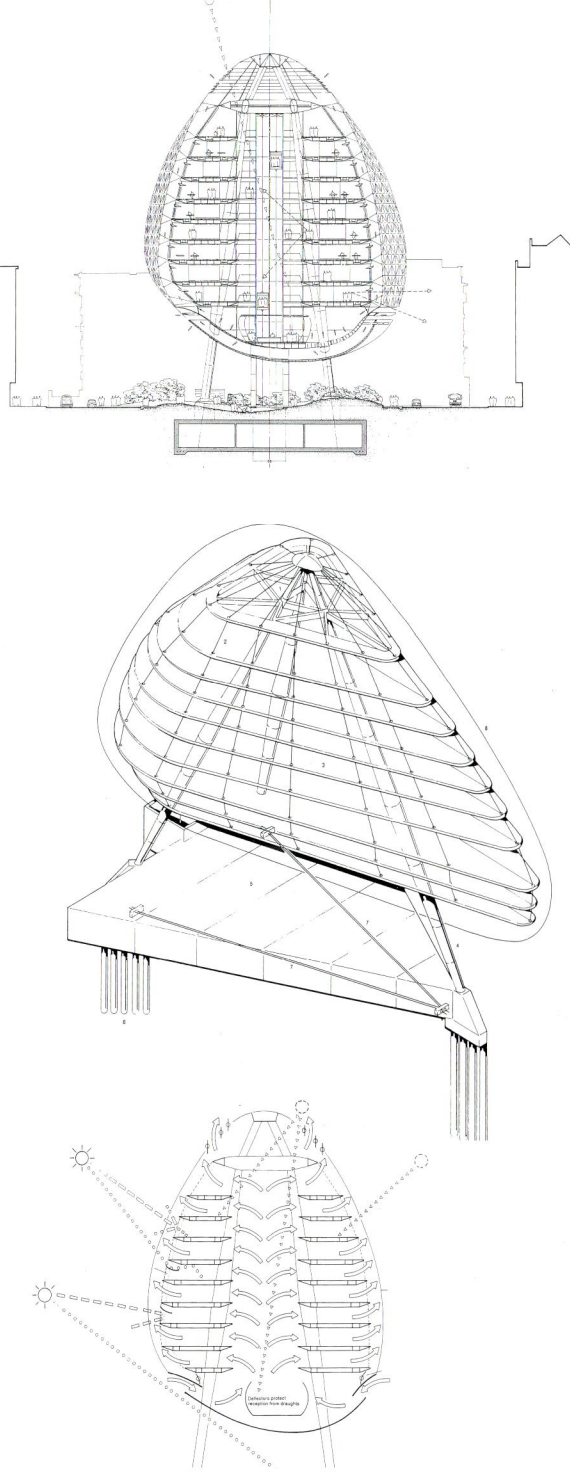

MAIN PICTURE: Model; ABOVE: Section; CENTRE: Diagram of structure; BELOW: Ventilation air flow pattern

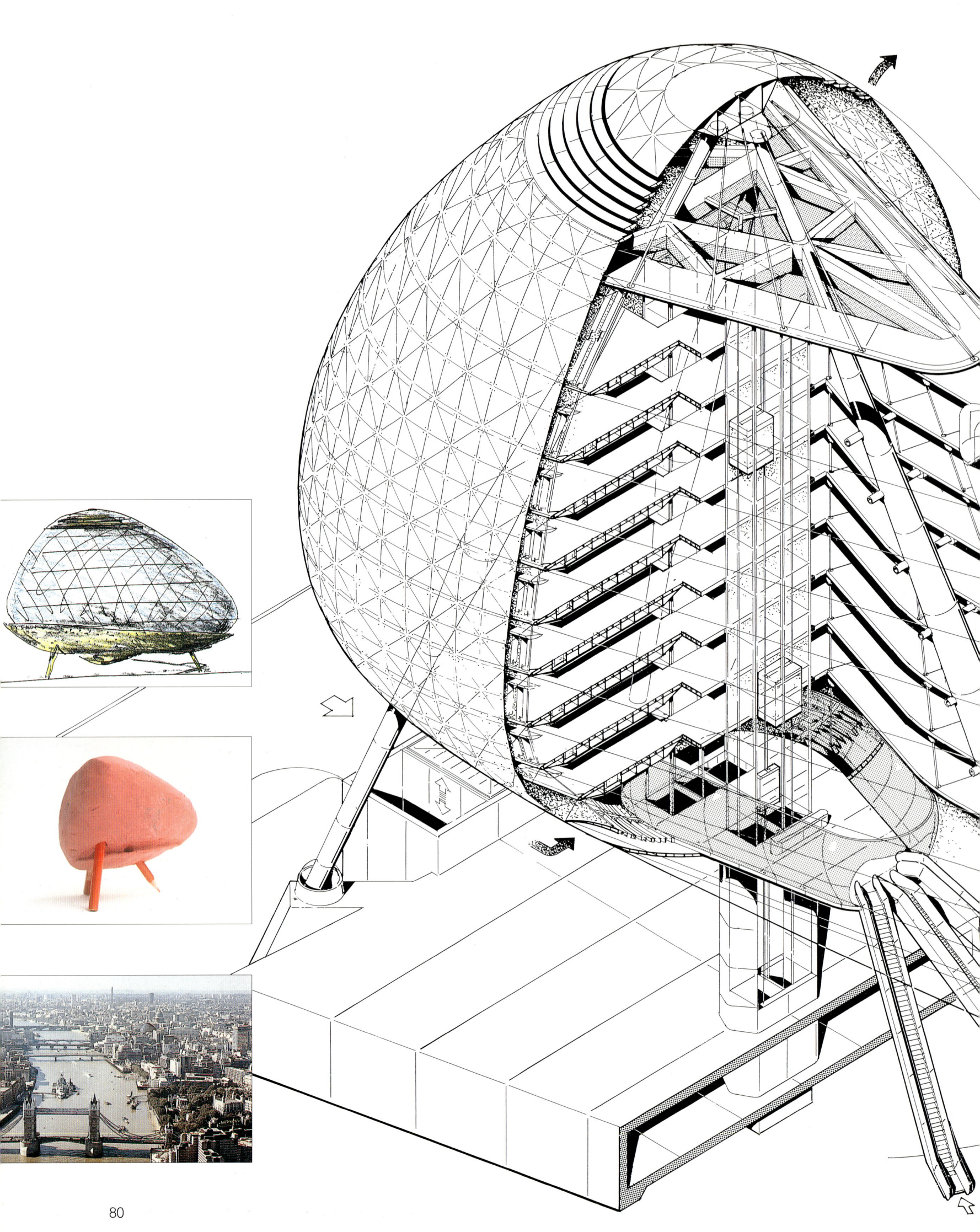

80

the entire facade within its own surface. The foundations to the tripod include a triangle of tie-beams between the feet of the tripod legs and groups of large diameter piles support the vertical loads from the building. Conventional naturally ventilated buildings use opening windows to create a crossflow of air for cooling. This system is not appropriate for inner-city buildings as noise pollution levels near open windows on the lower floors are unacceptable, consequently natural ventilation is often rejected. The Green Building uses a novel system of natural ventilation to achieve comfortable conditions for most of the year in the office spaces. Fresh, cool air is drawn into the building at the base of the atrium. Hot, stale air exhausts through louvres at the top of the building. Air intakes are 17 metres above ground level and at this height particulate and gaseous pollution levels are well below those at traffic level. An entirely glazed sealed outer skin and an inner skin of openable glass fins enables the air between to be heated by solar radiation. Air movement is created by the buoyancy of warm air and rises due to the 'stack' effect. In winter the thermal energy in the air can be recovered from the top of the building and used to preheat cold outside air at the bottom of the building to help offset building heat loss. Ventilation rates are controlled directly by the building users, who can open and close the inner skin of the building as with conventional windows. The fully sealed outer skin prevents uncontrolled entry of noise from the street. On windy days the form of the building helps reinforce the natural air flow patterns in the building. Air flowing over the top of the atrium creates a zone of negative pressure which helps pull hot air out of the building. A 'wind scoop' intercepts high velocity air falling down the faces of the building and directs it toward the air intakes leaving the garden below the building free from turbulence. Local cooling and heating can be provided at times of extreme external temperatures using a simple system of small heat pumps connected to a single 'tepid' water loop. This loop also allows the redistribution of energy from areas requiring cooling to those that require heating.

Natural light is a source of free illumination for a large part of the working year, and for many people it is psychologically preferable to artificial light. Unlike conventional deep plan offices the fully glazed facade of the Green Building allows natural light to enter from all directions. The open nature of the skin gives expansive views out, creating an important visual link between inside and outside. The highly glazed nature of the building, maximising the use of available sunlight, vastly reduces the amount of electrical energy required for artificial lighting as well as keeping the occupant 'in touch' with external weather conditions. The building profile is angled to allow maximum sunlight into the garden beneath the building. On overcast days, diffused light from the sky enters through the full height clear glazing. Artificial lighting can be switched off in all perimeter areas. Sky light also enters through the glazed top of the central atrium space. On days with bright sunshine fabric blinds can be lowered from within the second skin of the building to reduce solar heat gains and to control glare from the sun. These blinds are controlled locally by the occupants around the perimeter of the building. The second skin of the building incorporates a light directing element on each floor. A simple mechanism using flexible Mylar sheeting mirrors is used to reflect light into areas of the office furthest from the facade. The tilt angles of the Mylar mirrors are adjusted to re-direct incident sunlight into a horizontal plane just below the ceiling in each office. Satinised light deflectors are positioned below the ceiling in areas away from the facade to scatter the sunrays to floor level.

Architects: Future Systems; Structural & Service Engineers: Ove Arup & Partners

MAIN PICTURE: Cut away isometric; INSET, ABOVE TO BELOW: Sketch of building's shape; Basic model; View of London showing Green Building

VISITORS' CENTRE, STONEHENGE
Salisbury

With Stonehenge itself restored to its ancient empty plain, there remains the task of moderating the demands of the many thousands who wish to visit it. Our visitor centre is of the very present, not of the near or distant past. It is a low, smooth glass envelope, all but invisible from the monument itself, by design reflecting only the sky. Stretching across a wooded horizon it conceals the movement of people and vehicles, confining noise behind a timeless barrier. The first glimpse of the visitor centre from Stonehenge is of an abstract, primal and transparent form cut into the landscape, hinting at a physical presence.

The task of the centre is the interpretation of our prehistoric culture on Salisbury Plain. It addresses the paradox of Stonehenge, that it is being destroyed by the pilgrimage of millions. Our design addresses this tragic paradox by means of a paradox of its own: the concept of a no-building building. Stonehenge predates architecture, so our building must not evoke any period in time, rather it must be perceived as organic, growing from the landscape, echoing the gentle contours of the Plain. The landscape is our museum and our building is only a very small part of that landscape.

We have created a shallow grassed mound like the barrows of 5,000 years past. Into this barrow is set a clear glass lens viewed against the backdrop of trees and sky, a simple skeletal form barely visible from Stonehenge. The glass of the lens, like the stones, takes on the different lights and moods of the weather while ensuring that the building remains aloof from the monument, the low angles of the glass posing no crude challenge.

The internal environment of the building is created predominantly by natural means. The glazed roof collects both solar energy and rainwater, and provides natural light to the spaces below. The glazing consists of clear double glazed units incorporating a filter for ultra-violet light to prevent the fading of exhibits and furnishings below. A system of fish-like scales, profiled perforated panels with translucent insulation between, is suspended within the depth of the structure to protect the occupied spaces from direct sunlight and radiation. Air is extracted from the zone between the glazing and the scales, creating an effective buffer zone between the external climate and the internal environment. Fresh air is introduced into the building through an underfloor concrete plenum or hypocaust. In winter the building acts as a solar collector; solar energy trapped in the buffer zone beneath the glazing is drawn down to the occupied spaces by a mechanical extract system. The heavy construction of the hypocaust allows this heat to be stored within the building fabric for times when solar energy is insufficient. Make-up heat is provided from a gas fired installation heating the fresh supply air and perimeter heaters.

The materials chosen are simple, lasting and timeless. Glass is not only the oldest man-made material, but also one of the easiest surfaces to clean and maintain. The steel of the structure enables the sizes of the elements to be minimal and the stone floor throughout the building is the most lasting surface achievable. There are no walls, only partitions which can be rearranged and replaced as required.

A path suspended 400 millimetres above the downland penetrates the building, drawing people towards the monument across the Plain. Openings in this path allow wild grasses to grow below which will be trimmed by the pedestrian traffic. This line connects the centre with Stonehenge, whilst protecting the landscape from the millions of trampling feet.

Landscape Architects: Townshend Landscape Architects; Structural Engineers: YMR Anthony Hunt Associates; Services Engineers: Ove Arup & Partners; Quantity Surveyors: Davis Langdon & Everest

MAIN PICTURE: Model; OPPOSITE ABOVE: South elevation; INSET, ABOVE TO BELOW: Aerial view of the model; Aerial view of site; View of the path leading to the centre

PETER PRAN OF ELLERBE BECKET AND MICHAEL FIELDMAN
NEW YORK POLICE ACADEMY

The winning entry in an international competition for a new police academy, the design approach encompasses three main characteristics. Firstly, the ease with which it is operated and maintained; secondly, the support which the facility offers the users in its operations and daily routine; and thirdly, its innovative architecture must project itself through renewed recognition of the immeasurable impact the physical environment has on the well-being of its occupants and, of course, the building on fulfilment of its use. One of the aims has been to develop the most innovative architectural ideas of our time, coupled with the highest levels of design quality to generate an invigorating new architecture into the area that will become the beacon for a new standard. Two grids (or armatures) have been established and translated into two axes: axis one, academic spaces and axis two, physical training spaces. Mediating between the precision of these two axes are a series of support elements which have connections programmatically to both axes and at times, to public or visitor interaction. This includes administration and its symbolic role in directing all activities – mind and body related, as well as a series of special, more imposing spaces which include the museum, the auditorium and the library. The image of the building has succeeded in developing strength and movement in its architectural expression, while maintaining clarity of movement in and around the complex, so that the ease of use and fluid character of various components heighten the awareness of an enduring, dignified image befitting the seriousness of law enforcement.

Design Team: Peter Pran, Ed Calma, Andy Cers, Bill Chilton, Paul Davis, Timothy Johnson, Richard Varda, Dennis Wallace, Rodger Goodhill; Michael Fieldman & Partners: Michael Fieldman, Miles Cigolle, Andrew Heidig, Elissa Icso, Jyh-Meei Jong, John Jordan, Ed Rawlings

MAIN PICTURE: Model; OPPOSITE, ABOVE TO BELOW: Level 8 Floor Plan; Level 3 Floor Plan; East elevation; THIS PAGE: Site plan

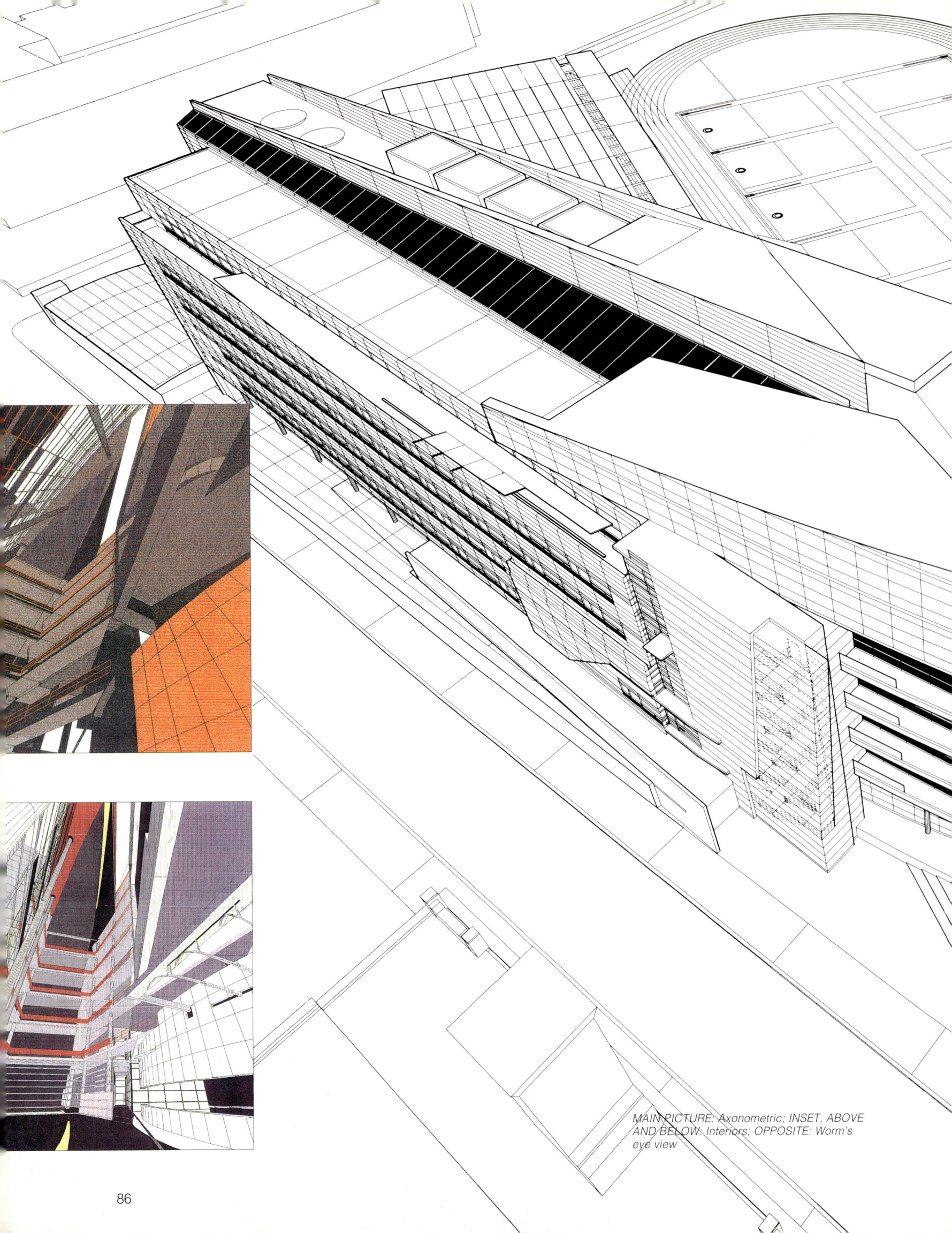

MAIN PICTURE: Axonometric; INSET, ABOVE AND BELOW: Interiors; OPPOSITE: Worm's eye view

HAJIME YATSUKA
NI-IGATA CIVIC CENTRE
Japan

The centre is a complex which includes an auditorium with 2,000 seats, a theatre of 900 seats, a Noh theatre with 350 seats and the accompanying auxiliary facilities. The site is situated in the centre of the cultural sports park of Ni-igata city in North Japan. It also faces Japan's longest river, the Shinano. The park has suffered from the absence of a coherent and convincing building setting. The riverside is one of the most attractive places but the view had been cut off from the rest of the park by roads. Our primary concern was to give a sense of integration and continuity to this confusing context by superimposing a huge artificial slope of boomerang shape to include the requested facilities. Above this plateau you can see the roofs of the halls and two prominent structures which are the highlights of the complex. The first is constructed with fine steel lattices to include a belvedere with a tiny tea house in the air. The second is a steel column 100 metres high, called a 'cloud supporter'. Suspended from it is a long spiral ramp which provides access to the belvedere. The whole structure is motivated by a sense of movement rising towards heaven. It is dedicated to my hero, Ivan Leonidov.

MAIN PICTURE: Model; INSET, ABOVE TO BELOW: Perspective of lobby; North elevation; South elevation

NASUNOGAHARA HARMONY HALL
Japan

This project consists of an auditorium with 1,350 seats, a theatre with 400 seats and a contemporary art gallery. The location lacks any significant contextual character since it is situated in a rice field surrounded by farm houses. Imposing a monumental or deconstructive mass onto this landscape was deemed to be rather ridiculous, so the building was submerged four metres in order to reduce the volume exposed to the outside. The design is introversive, focusing on the central sunken landscape with its curved slope. This central garden separates the two halls and gallery space, turning the conventional relationship of figure (building) to ground (landscape) inside out. Both landscape and buildings are integrated as an ever changing fluidal order. The entrance pavilion is an immobile rock with a raised amphitheatre on top. The glass facade of a hall wing is also treated as a fluid.

MAIN PICTURE: Model; ABOVE LEFT: West elevation; ABOVE RIGHT: South elevation

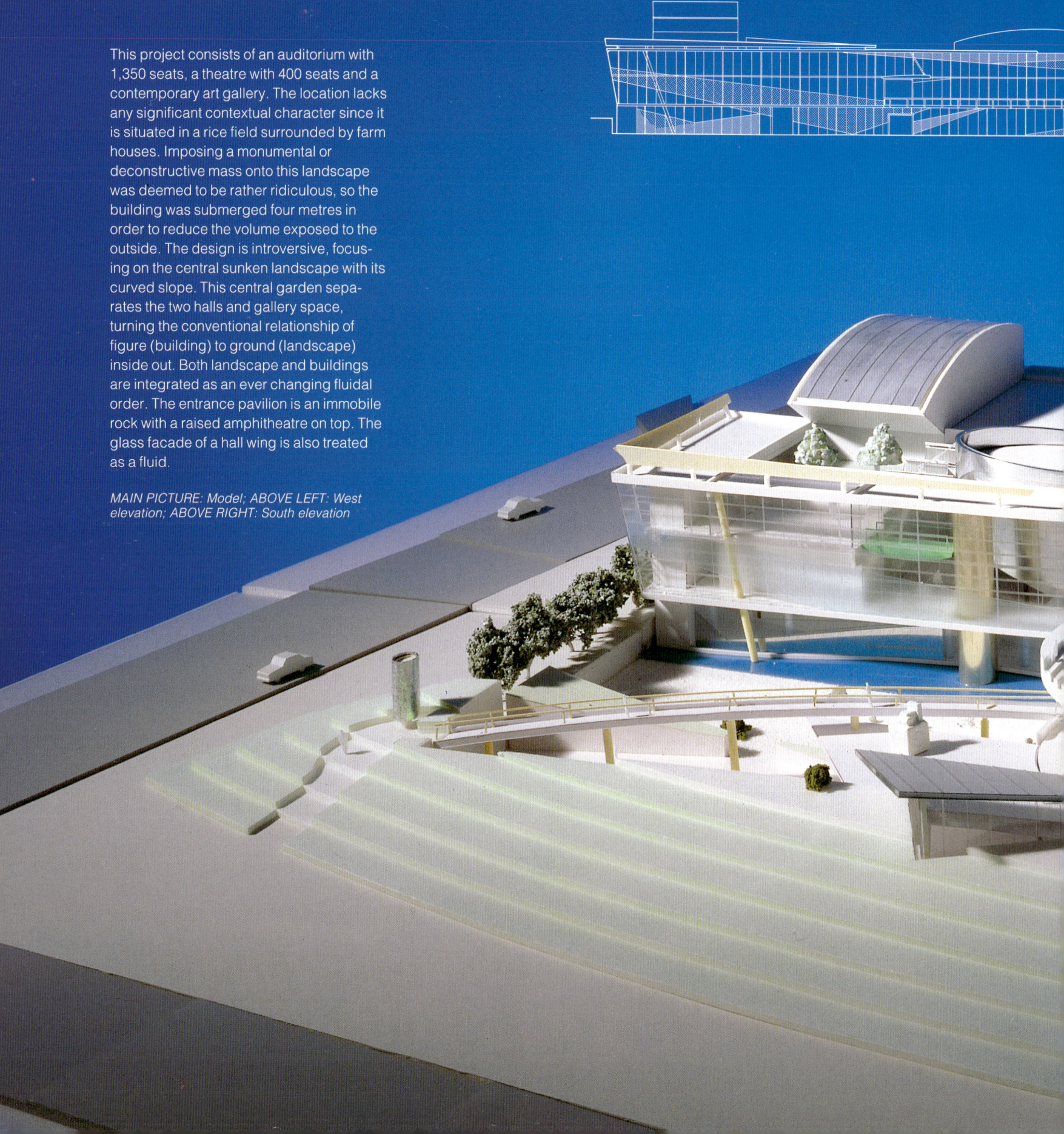

KIKO MOZUNA
NOTOJIMA GLASS ART MUSEUM

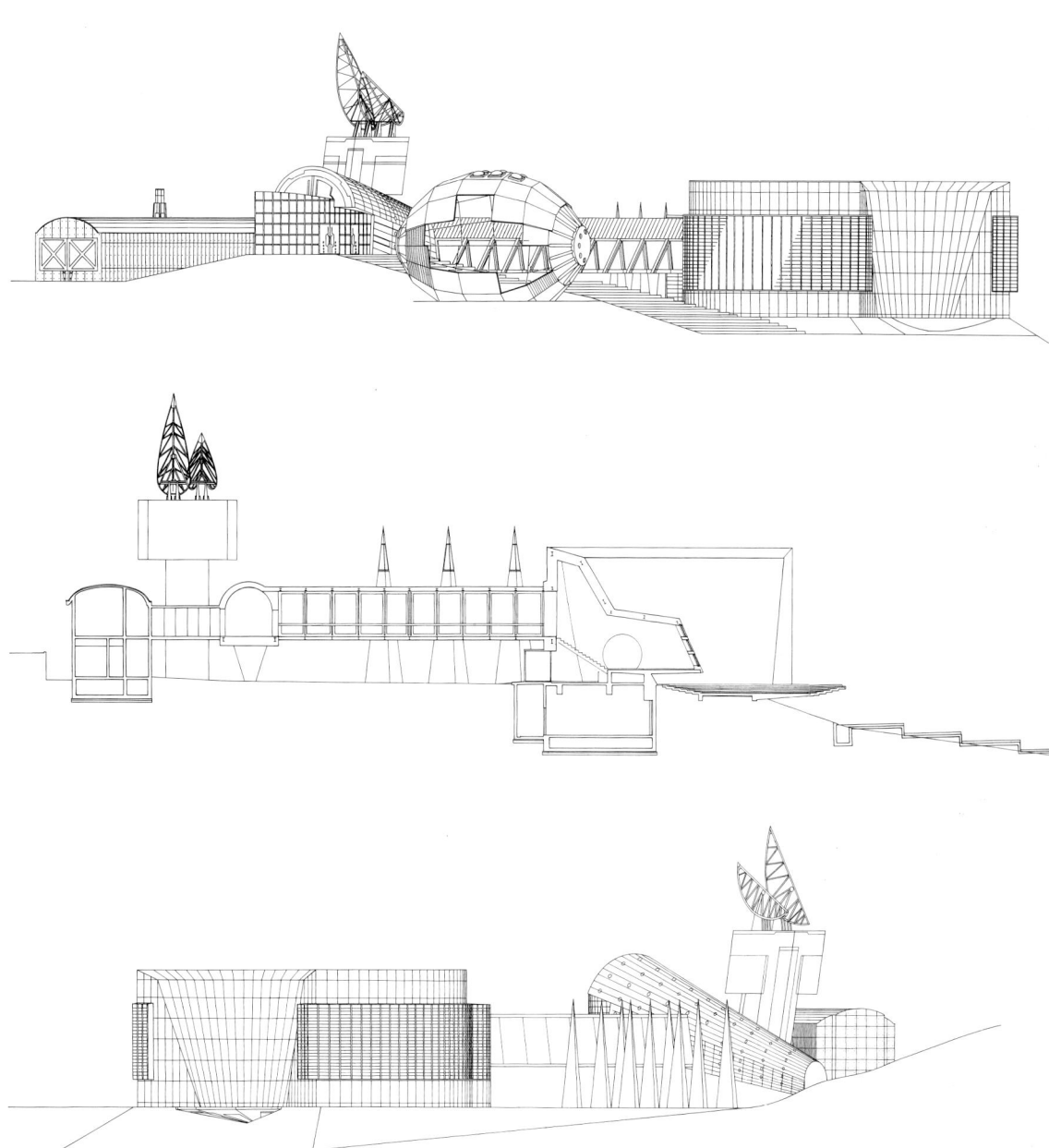

The theme of this project is the City of Glass; harmonising architecture, mankind and the environment, with three sub-concepts: Four Guardian Gods (*shishinsoou*); the Dry Garden (*karesansui*); and Neo-Orientalism (*wakonyoosai*).

Four Guardian Gods in oriental symbolism means geography and directions to be the sacred guardians of a city, and many great cities have applied this vision in order to ensure their prosperity.

In the Glass Art Museum project, the basic composition and zoning are made up following this concept of four different programmes: permanent exhibition space, second exhibition space, office and shop space and open exhibition space.

The Dry Garden is an abstraction of the structure of nature in the form of a garden, which allows any landscape or geographical dimensions to be projected into the pure cosmological order. This method of interconnecting artifacts and nature can be applied to establish the harmony between environment (marginal) and architecture (design), in an attempt to reconstitute the original image of landscape.

In this project, the area itself is conceived as an enormous dry garden, where each scattered construction serves as a poetic link to enhance enjoyment of the varied architectonic landscape, and to modify the whole amenity, including its highlight – the artificial pond in the middle of the permanent exhibition space – which is assimilated with the background of the Noto Sea.

Neo-Orientalism tries to integrate Japanese concepts with a more occidental style in a modern interpretation which places our traditional background in a future context. The gate, entrances and passages are designed on the basis of a combination of traditional Japanese factors with fractal geometry using up-to-date materials.

Engineers: Murakami Structure & Engineering, Sakurai System

ABOVE: Front elevation; CENTRE: Cross section; BELOW: Rear elevation; OPPOSITE: Detail of interior; INSET, ABOVE TO BELOW: Interior and exterior views; OVERLEAF: Exhibition space